RAF, DOMINION & ALLIED SQUADRONS AT WAR:
STUDY, HISTORY AND STATISTICS

COMPILED BY
PHIL H. LISTEMANN

Drawings by Clavework-graphics

PREFACE

The purpose of this study is to provide aviation historians and enthusiasts with a range of information relative to each of the Commonwealth squadrons that saw combat during World War II. Each record will comprise a short history, complete with illustrations and artwork, and accompanied by the following appendices:

Appendix I: Squadron Commanders and Flight Commanders
Appendix II: Major awards
Appendix III: Operational diary (number of sorties per month)
Appendix IV: Victory list
Appendix V: Aircraft losses on operations
Appendix VI: Aircraft losses in accidents
Appendix VII: Aircraft Serial numbers matching with individual letters (including mission totals for multi-engine aircraft)
Appendix VIII: Nominal roll (Captains only for bomber and seaplane units)
Appendix IX: Roll of Honour

Individual files will be constantly updated, when any fresh information comes to light. Additional information will be available for download, at no charge, on each squadron's site at:

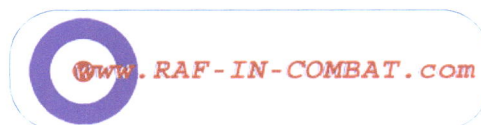

www.RAF-IN-COMBAT.com

GLOSSARY OF TERMS

RANKS

AC: Aircraftman
G/C: Group Captain
W/C: Wing Commander
S/L: Squadron Leader
F/L: Flight Lieutenant
F/O: Flying Officer
P/O: Pilot Officer
W/O: Warrant Officer
F/Sgt: Flight Sergeant
Sgt: Sergeant
Cpl: Corporal
LAC: Leading Aircraftman

DFM: Distinguished Flying Medal
DSO: Distinguished Service Order
Eva.: Evaded
Inj.: Injured
ORB: Operational Record Book
OTU: Operational Training Unit
PAF: Polish Air Force
PoW: Prisoner of War
RAF: Royal Air Force
RAAF: Royal Australian Air Force
RCAF: Royal Canadian Air Force
RNZAF: Royal New Zealand Air Force
SAAF: South African Air Force
Sqn: Squadron
TOC: Taken on charge
†: Killed

OTHER

AAF: Auxiliary Air Force
CO: Commanding Officer
DFC: Distinguished Flying Cross

No. 452 (RAAF) Squadron 1941-1945

ISBN: 978-2918590-74-3

Contributors & Acknowledgments:

Aviation Heritage Museum of WA, Drew Harrison, Malcolm Laird

Stephen McGregor (The Spitfire Association - Australia), Steve Mackenzie, Andrew Thomas

Cover: Spitfire Mk.VIII A58-516 usually flown by F/O Kenneth May flying around Morotai (NEI) in December 1944.

MAIN EQUIPMENT

SPITFIRE I	Apr.41 - May.41
SPITFIRE II	May.41 - Aug.41
SPITFIRE V	Aug.41 - May.42
	Sept.42 - Jun.44
SPITFIRE VIII	Jan.44 - Nov.45

SQUADRON CODE LETTERS:

UD
(EUROPE)

QY
(AUSTRALIA FROM JUNE 1943 AND PACIFIC)

SQUADRON HISTORY

No. 452 (RAAF) Squadron was the first Australian squadron formed in Britain during the Second World War. It came into being at Kirton-in-Lindsey on **8 April 1941** under the command of Squadron Leader Roy Dutton, a very experienced British pilot. After working up on war-weary Spitfire Mk.I's, it became operational in May with Spitfire Mk.II's and performed its first sorties on 22nd when Sergeants Milnes and Roberts took off to patrol off the coast. Until the move to Kenley in July, the squadron flew mainly convoy patrols and a few unconclusive interceptions. However things changed with first offensive sweep over France on 11 July. On this occasion the Irish flight commander 'Paddy' Finucane shot down the squadron's first German aircraft. Unfortunately one aircraft and pilot were also lost to the Germans during the same engagement.

From that day forth No.452 Squadron rapidly developed a formidable reputation on operations against the Luftwaffe; especially after the squadron relinquished its venerable Spitfire Mk.IIs for Spitfire Mk.Vs in August 1941. It went on to claim 69 confirmed or probable victories through to mid-March 1942, but sustained in return rather heavy losses; 23 aircraft in combats that claimed the lives of 12 pilots, while 6 more became prisoners. Some of these were due to multiple losses on single missions, including four during a 18 September 1941 engagement.

The tally of some pilots became very impressive. While 'Paddy' Finucane was the most successful pilot of that time, Australians like 'Throttle' Thorold-Smith, 'Bluey' Truscott or Keith Chisholm also scored consistently. Logically awards followed as squadron members were awarded a DSO, eight DFC or Bars to DFC, and one DFM in the same period.

However, the situation changed a little later in the spring of 1942 when it was determined that Australia needed fighter squadrons to defend its own cities located in the north. Among the three Fighter Command units chosen to be sent to Australia, No.452 and its sister unit, No.457 (RAAF) Squadron, were natural selections. However to allow the latter to gain combat experience before sailing to Australia, No.452 was witdrawn from operations in March 1942. It eventually sailed for home on 21 June 1942, arriving in Melbourne on 13 August and re-assembled at Richmond, New South Wales on 6 September without aircraft (which were in the Middle East on route.) After refresher training on various aircraft, No.452 Squadron became operational on Spitfires again in January 1943 at Batchelor, Northern Territory. Here, along with No.54 (RAF) and No.457 (RAAF) Squadrons, it became part of No.1 Fighter Wing, RAAF with the main task of defending Darwin.

About one year after its last victory in Europe No.452 Sqn claimed two Japanese aircraft during a raid on Darwin but lost its CO, S/L 'Throttle' Thorold-Smith, during the engagement. Throughout the next few months the squadron was involved in many defensive actions, and although they claimed 18 more victories against the Japanese, they also suffered heavy losses.

In March 1944, it moved south to defend Perth but little action was recorded. In May it became part of No.80 Fighter Wing, RAAF. No.452 Sqn returned north in July 1944, re-equipped with Spitfire Mk.VIIIs, and became employed in the ground attack role for the rest of the war. In December 1944 it joined the 1st Tactical Air Force and relocated to Morotai in the Dutch East Indies to support Australian operations in Borneo. The squadron's Spitfires moved to Balikpapan on 15 July 1945, following the landings there earlier in the month, and flew in support of the land campaign. Its last victory of the war was claimed nine days later. With the dropping of the atomic bombs in August, the squadron's days were numbered. It flew its last operational sortie of the on 10 August, and was subsequently disbanded on **17 November 1945** at Tarakan.

ARTICLE XV

Shortly after Britain's declaration of war, supported on the same date by Australia and New Zealand, and Canada a week later, the British Government asked Commonwealth countries to supply partially trained aircrew for the expansion of the RAF. In those years prior to the war an allocation of men from the Dominions had been offered Short Service, or Permanent, Commission in the RAF, but the speed with which the Nazis had overrun Poland, made it clear that large numbers of airmen would be needed urgently. In November 1939, the Ottawa (Canada) Conference formulated the setting-up of the Empire Air Training Scheme (EATS) to train aircrew to a uniform standard in each of the Dominions previously mentioned, and subsequently South Africa, which was already operating a scheme, and Rhodesia.

Desirous of exercising some control over its own nationals, which was not the case for those who had joined up prior to the war, Canada obtained, via Article XV, an agreement that their aircrew would be gathered together in national squadrons, to serve alongside the permanent units of the RAF. For operational and administrative reasons Australia and New Zealand were reluctant to establish and maintain RAAF or RNZAF squadrons in Britain so eventually it was decided that units formed in the RAF would be identified with them.

In order to distinguish those units created under Article XV the RAF reserved a block of numbers commencing with 400 which was allocated to them. The RCAF squadrons were to start with 400, the RAAF, 450 and the RNZAF, 485. From the start aircrew were paid at the rates of pay in force in their respective countries, and depended on the RAF for aircraft and logistical support.

Their operational deployment was to be determined by the RAF, even though respective Governments of each of the Dominions retained an overview on their airmen. Some existing squadrons were re-numbered in the new series to avoid confusion with established RAF units. As an example No.1 Squadron RCAF, which was sent to support Great Britain in 1940, was subsequently re-numbered No.401 (RCAF) Squadron. The policy behind Article XV Squadrons provided a greater national identity to those countries who were able to identify themselves in their title e.g. No.452 (RAAF) Squadron.

Initially the RAF supplied the vast majority of the ground personnel for most of the Commonwealth squadrons. The aircrew posted to these squadrons represented only some, and not all, of that particular country's nationals. Indeed almost every squadron in the RAF at some time or another had members amongst their ranks from all of the Dominions - aircrew were sent where there was the greatest need for them.

In the beginning the authorities attempted to relocate serving RAF officers to those newly formed squadrons from their Dominions. However this was not always possible or practical, especially where senior positions needed to be filled. As a result British or other nationals frequently filled the vacancies in these squadrons. Regrettably friction between nationalities sometimes occurred, although this was not a major problem. The posting or replacement of certain personnel would generally defuse such situations.

By the end of the war Article XV Squadrons had proved that they were equal to the best that the RAF had produced and had no need to be envious of their British counterparts. Not only had they achieved impressive operational records but they gave the Dominions a renewed confidence and pride in their military ability.

Of the Dominions Australia became the second biggest contributor after Canada, providing 17 operational squadrons between 1941 and 1943, six were of the day-fighter type (by the end of the war). Furthermore, two more RAAF squadrons fought under RAF authority all war long, Nos.3 and 10.

Kirton-in-Lindsey	08.04.41 - 21.07.41	Batchelor	17.01.43 - 01.02.43
Kenley	21.07.41 - 21.10.41	Strauss	01.02.43 - 11.03.44
Redhill	21.10.41 - 14.01.42	Guildford	11.03.44 - 25.03.44
Kenley	14.01.42 - 23.03.42	Strauss	25.03.44 - 01.07.44
Andreas	23.03.42 - 18.06.42	Sattler	01.07.44 - 11.12.44
En route to Australia	-	Morotai (NEI)	11.12.44 - 29.06.45
Melbourne	13.08.42 - 06.09.42	Tarakan (NEI)	29.06.45 - 17.11.45
Mascot	06.09.42 - 17.01.43		

APPENDIX I
Squadron and Flight Commanders

Rank and Name	SN	Origin	Dates
S/L Roy G. **Dutton**	RAF No.33072	RAF	13.04.41 - 15.06.41
S/L Robert W. **Bungey**	RAF No.40042	(AUS)/RAF	15.06.41 - 26.01.42
S/L Keith W. **Truscott**	Aus.400213	RAAF	26.01.42 - 18.03.42
S/L Raymond E. **Thorold-Smith** *(†)*	Aus.402144	RAAF	18.03.42 - 15.03.43
S/L Ronald S. **MacDonald**	Aus.270812	RAAF	18.03.43 - 03.02.44
S/L Louis T. **Spence**	Aus.270839	RAAF	03.02.44 - 28.11.44
S/L Arthur H. **Birch**	Aus.402719	RAAF	28.11.44 - 04.06.45
S/L Kevin M. **Barclay**	Aus.407662	RAAF	04.06.45 - 12.09.45
F/L William **Friend** *(Temp.)*	Aus.403328	RAAF	12.09.45 - 17.10.45

A Flight

F/L Brendan E.F. **Finucane**	RAF No.41276	(IRE)/RAF	13.04.41 - 15.10.41
F/L Raymond E. **Thorold-Smith**	Aus.402144	RAAF	15.10.41 - 18.03.42
F/L John R. **Ross** *(†)*	Aus.400157	RAAF	18.03.42 - 20.10.42
F/L Edward S. **Hall**	Aus.403013	RAAF	02.01.43 - 26.07.43
F/L Davidson F. **Evans**	Aus.404724	RAAF	26.07.43 - 19.11.43
F/L Keith M. **Gamble**	Aus.403049	RAAF	19.11.43 - 14.09.44
F/L Keith D. **Cotton**	Aus.411484	RAAF	14.09.44 - 18.04.45
F/O Jack A. **Pretty**	Aus.409220	RAAF	18.04.45 - 20.09.45

B Flight

F/L Alfred G. **Douglas**	RAF No.70188	RAF	08.05.41 - 29.09.41
F/L Keith W. **Truscott**	Aus.400213	RAAF	29.09.41 - 26.01.42
F/L Frank A. **Cocker**	Aus.403858	RAAF	26.01.42 - 16.02.42
F/L Clive N. **Wawn**	Aus.400163	RAAF	16.02.42 - 18.03.42
F/L Raymond H.C. **Sly**	Aus.402260	RAAF	18.03.42 - 23.03.42
F/L Paul St.J. **Makin**	RAF No.116507	(AUS)/RAF	23.03.42 - 29.07.43
F/L John H.E. **Bisley**	Aus.402720	RAAF	29.07.43 - 29.01.44
F/L Ronald W. **Cundy**	Aus.402732	RAAF	29.01.44 - 13.09.44
F/L Desmond J. **Cormack**	Aus.402732	RAAF	13.09.44 - 15.05.45
F/L William **Friend**	Aus.403328	RAAF	15.05.45 - 17.10.45

APPENDIX II
Major Awards

DSO: 1
Brendan Eamonn Fergus **Finucane** (RAF No.41276 - RAF), *Ireland*

DFC: 9

*including 2 First Bar: * and 1 Second Bar:***

Robert Wilton **Bungey** (RAF No.40042 - RAF), *AUSTRALIA*
Desmond John **Cormack** (Aus.407412 - RAAF)
Brendan Eamonn Fergus **Finucane** (RAF No.41276 - RAF)*, *IRELAND*
Brendan Eamonn Fergus **Finucane** (RAF No.41276 - RAF)**, *IRELAND*
Jack Emerson **Pretty** (Aus.409220 - RAAF)
Raymond Edward **Thorold-Smith** (Aus.402144 - RAAF)
Keith William **Truscott** (Aus.400213 - RAAF)
Keith William **Truscott** (Aus.400213 - RAAF)*
Clive Newton **Wawn** (Aus.400163 - RAAF)

DFM: 1

Keith Bruce **Chisholm** (Aus.402150 - RAAF)

APPENDIX III
OPERATIONAL DIARY
NUMBER OF SORTIES PER MONTH

Date	Month	Total	Date	Month	Total
May.41	10	10	Aug.43	54	1,954
Jun.41	127	137	Sep.43	52	2,006
Jul.41	201	338	Oct.43	6	2,012
Aug.41	293	631	Nov.43	12	2,024
Sep.41	146	777	Dec.43	-	2,024
Oct.41	109	886	Jan.44	38	2,062
Nov.41	79	965	.../...		
Dec.41	63	1,028	Apr.44	44	2,106
Jan.42	75	1,103	May.44	22	2,128
Feb.42	82	1,185	Jun.44	15	2,143
Mar.42	98	1,283	.../...		
Apr.42	76	1,359	Dec.44	111	2,254
May.42	66	1,425	Jan.45	315	2,569
.../...			Feb.45	162	2,731
Jan.43	4	1,429	Mar.45	125	2,856
Feb.43	56	1,485	Apr.45	89	2,945
Mar.43	115	1,600	May.45	-	2,945
Apr.43	12	1,612	Jun.45	4	2,949
May.43	79	1,697	Jul.45	127	3,076
Jun.43	104	1,801	Aug.45	25	3,101
Jul.43	99	1,900			
			Grand Total		**3,101**

Extracted from AIR27/1892 & Form A.50-A.51

APPENDIX IV
VICTORY LIST
CONFIRMED (C) AND PROBABLE (P) CLAIMS

Date	Pilot	SN	Origin	Type	Serial	Code	Nb	Cat.
		SPITFIRE II						
11.07.41	F/L Brendan E.F. **Finucane**	RAF No.41276	(IRE)/RAF	Bf109	**P8038**		1.0	C
24.07.41	F/O Andrew H. **Humphrey**	RAF No.33543	RAF	Bf109	**P7973**		1.0	C

03.08.41	F/L Brendan E.F. **Finucane**	RAF No.41276	(IRE)/RAF	Bf109	**P8038**		1.0	C
	P/O William D. **Eccleton**	Aus.402232	RAAF	Bf109	**P8264**		1.0	C
	F/L Brendan E.F. **Finucane**	RAF No.41276	(IRE)/RAF	Bf109	**P8038**		1.0	P
09.08.41	F/L Brendan E.F. **Finucane**	RAF No.41276	(IRE)/RAF	Bf109	**P8038**		1.0	C
	F/L Brendan E.F. **Finucane**	RAF No.41276	(IRE)/RAF	Bf109	**P8038**		0.5	C
	P/O Raymond E. **Thorold-Smith**	Aus.402144	RAAF		**P8381**		0.5	C
	P/O Donald E. **Lewis**	Aus.402148	RAAF	Bf109	**P7853**	UD-Y	0.5	C
	Sgt Keith B. **Chisholm**	Aus.402150	RAAF		**P7786**	UD-C	0.5	C
	F/L Brendan E.F. **Finucane**	RAF No.41276	(IRE)/RAF	Bf109	**P8038**		0.5	C
	Sgt Keith B. **Chisholm**	Aus.402150	RAAF		**P7786**	UD-C	0.5	C
	P/O Keith W. **Truscott**	Aus.400213	RAAF	Bf109	**P7973**		1.0	C
16.08.41	F/L Brendan E.F. **Finucane**	RAF No.41276	(IRE)/RAF	Bf109	**P8170**		2.0	C
	Sgt Archibald R. **Stuart**	Aus.402141	RAAF	Bf109	**P8518**	RF-J*	1.0	C
19.08.41	F/L Brendan E.F. **Finucane**	RAF No.41276	(IRE)/RAF	Bf109	**P8170**		1.0	C
	F/L Brendan E.F. **Finucane**	RAF No.41276	(IRE)/RAF	Bf109	**P8170**		1.0	P
26.08.41	Sgt Archibald R. **Stuart**	Aus.402141	RAAF	Bf109	**P8148**	UD-F	1.0	C

*Personal aircraft of W/C John Kent

SPITFIRE V

16.08.41	F/L Brendan E.F. **Finucane**	RAF No.41276	(IRE)/RAF	Bf109	**AB852**	UD-W	1.0	C
	P/O Keith W. **Truscott**	Aus.400213	RAAF	Bf109	**AB792**		1.0	C
	Sgt Eric B. **Tainton**	Aus.402009	RAAF	Bf109	**W3572**		1.0	C
	Sgt Keith B. **Chisholm**	Aus.402150	RAAF		**W3571**		2.0	C
19.08.41	P/O Keith W. **Truscott**	Aus.400213	RAAF	Bf109	**AB792**		1.0	P
26.08.41	F/L Albert G. **Douglas**	RAF No.70188	RAF	Bf109	**W3646**		1.0	C
27.08.41	P/O Raymond E. **Thorold-Smith**	Aus.402144	RAAF	Bf109	**P8717**		2.0	C
	F/L Brendan E.F. **Finucane**	RAF No.41276	(IRE)/RAF	Bf109	**AB852**	UD-W	2.0	C
02.09.41	P/O William D. **Willis**	Aus.402166	RAAF	Bf109	**W3605**		1.0	C
	Sgt Archibald R. **Stuart**	Aus.402141	RAAF	Bf109	**P8708**		1.0	C
18.09.41	F/L Albert G. **Douglas**	RAF No.70188	RAF	Bf109	**AB842**		1.0	C
	P/O Raymond E. **Thorold-Smith**	Aus.402144	RAAF	Bf109	**AB852**	UD-W	1.0	C
	Sgt Keith B. **Chisholm**	Aus.402150	RAAF	Bf109	**W3520**		1.0	C
	P/O Keith W. **Truscott**	Aus.400213	RAAF	Bf109	**AB781**		1.0	C
				Bf109	**AB781**		1.0	P
20.09.41	Sgt Keith B. **Chisholm**	Aus.402150	RAAF	Bf109	**W3520**		1.0	C
	F/L Brendan E.F. **Finucane**	RAF No.41276	(IRE)/RAF	Bf109	**AB852**	UD-W	3.0	C
	P/O Keith W. **Truscott**	Aus.400213	RAAF	Bf109	**W3605**	UD-N	2.0	C
	Sgt Bruce P. **Dunstan**	RAF No.1256932	(AUS)/RAF	Bf109	**W3529**		1.0	C
21.09.41	P/O Keith W. **Truscott**	Aus.400213	RAAF	Bf109	**AB792**	UD-M	1.0	C
	Sgt Clive N. **Wawn**	Aus.400163	RAAF	Bf109	**AB842**		1.0	C
	F/L Brendan E.F. **Finucane**	RAF No.41276	(IRE)/RAF	Bf109	**AB852**	UD-W	2.0	C
	Sgt Keith B. **Chisholm**	Aus.402150	RAAF	Bf109	**W3520**		1.0	C
02.10.41	Sgt Raife J. **Cowan**	Aus.404087	RAAF	Bf109	**W3520**		1.0	C
	F/L Brendan E.F. **Finucane**	RAF No.41276	(IRE)/RAF	Bf109	**AB972**		1.0	C
12.10.41	F/L Brendan E.F. **Finucane**	RAF No.41276	(IRE)/RAF	Bf109	**AB972**		1.0	C
	F/L Keith W. **Truscott**	Aus.400213	RAAF	Bf109	**AB842**		1.0	P
13.10.41	F/L Keith W. **Truscott**	Aus.400213	RAAF	Bf109	**AB842**		2.0	C
	Sgt John M. **Emery**	Aus.407116	RAAF	Bf109	**AB966**		1.0	C
	P/O Eric H. **Schrader**	Aus.400135	RAAF	Bf109	**AD242**	UD-E	1.0	C
	F/L Brendan E.F. **Finucane**	RAF No.41276	(IRE)/RAF	Bf109	**AB972**		2.0	C
	P/O Raymond E. **Thorold-Smith**	Aus.402144	RAAF	Bf109	**W3821**	UD-D	1.0	C
06.11.41	F/L Raymond E. **Thorold-Smith**	Aus.402144	RAAF	Fw190	**W3821**	UD-D	1.0	C
				Bf109	**W3821**	UD-D	1.0	C
	F/L Keith W. **Truscott**	Aus.400213	RAAF	Bf109	**AB376**		1.0	C
	S/L Robert W. **Bungey**	RAF No.40042	(AUS)/RAF	Bf109	**AB857**		1.0	C
08.11.41	F/L Keith W. **Truscott**	Aus.400213	RAAF	Bf109	**AB842**		2.0	C
09.03.42	F/L Clive N. **Wawn**	Aus.400163	RAAF	Bf109	**BL744**	UD-U	1.0	C
				Bf109	**BL744**	UD-U	1.0	P
	F/L Keith W. **Truscott**	Aus.400213	RAAF	Bf109	**AB994**	UD-M	1.0	C

13.03.42	P/O Raymond H.C. **Sly**	Aus.402260	RAAF	Fw190	**AB260**		1.0	C
14.03.42	Sgt John McA. **Morrison**	Aus.402522	RAAF	Bf109	**AB185**		1.0	P
	F/L Keith W. **Truscott**	Aus.400213	RAAF	Fw190	**AB994**	UD-M	1.0	C
15.03.43	F/O Adrian P. **Goldsmith**	Aus.402500	RAAF	A6M	**BR526**	J	1.0	C
				G4M	**BR526**	J	1.0	C
02.05.43	F/O Granville A. **Mawer**	Aus.403112	RAAF	'Zeke'	**BS236**		1.0	C
	F/O Adrian P. **Goldsmith**	Aus.402500	RAAF	G4M	**BR526**	J	1.0	C
	F/O Davidson F. **Evans**	Aus.404724	RAAF	'Zeke'	**BR240**		1.0	C
20.06.43	F/O John H.E. **Bisley**	Aus.402720	RAAF	Sally	**BS236**		1.0	C
	F/O Granville A. **Mawer**	Aus.403112	RAAF	'Zeke'	**BR548**	M	1.0	C
	S/L Ronald S. **MacDonald**	Aus.270812	RAAF	'Sally'	**BR574**	D	1.0	C
	F/O Davidson F. **Evans**	Aus.404724	RAAF	'Sally'	**AR563**	R	1.0	C
	F/Sgt Anthony T. **Ruskin-Rowe**	Aus.411389	RAAF	'Sally'	**BS174**	W	1.0	P
30.06.43	F/L Edward S. **Hall**	Aus.403013	RAAF	'Zeke'	**BS186**	L	1.0	C
	F/Sgt Colin R. **Duncan**	Aus.401778	RAAF	'Betty'	**AR523**	A	1.0	P
	P/O Paul D. **Tully**	Aus.404998	RAAF	'Betty'	**BS186**	L	0.5	C
	F/O Gerald J. **Cowell**	Aus.400967	RAAF		**EE672**		0.5	C
06.07.43	S/L Ronald S. **MacDonald**	Aus.270812	RAAF	'Betty'	**BS236**		1.0	C
	F/O Clive P. **Lloyd**	Aus.404690	RAAF	'Zeke'	**BR549**	QY-K	1.0	C
	P/O Paul D. **Tully**	Aus.404998	RAAF	'Zeke'	**ES367**		1.0	C
10.08.43	F/O Frederick J. **Young**	Aus.403777	RAAF	'Pete'	**EE672**		0.5	C
	P/O William M. **Coombes**	Aus.403800	RAAF		**BS186**	QY-L	0.5	C
07.09.43	F/L Adrian P. **Goldsmith**	Aus.402500	RAAF	'Tony'	**JL378**	QY-Y	1.0	C
	F/O Gerald J. **Cowell**	Aus.400967	RAAF	'Oscar'	**BS236**		1.0	C
12.06.44	F/O Keith M. **Gamble**	Aus.400349	RAAF	'Dinah'	**A58-248**		0.33	C
	F/O Colin H. **O'Laughlin**	Aus.407449	RAAF		**A58-117**		0.33	C
	F/O Malcolm J. **Beaton**	Aus.417787	RAAF		**A58-228**		0.33	C

Spitfire VIII

24.12.44	F/O Jack A. **Pretty**	Aus.409220	RAAF	'Nick'	**A58-518**	QY-O	1.0	C
24.07.45	F/O Jeffrey C. **King**	Aus.401823	RAAF	'Helen'	**A58-430**	QY-V	1.0	C

Total: 91.0

Aircraft damaged: 29.0

APPENDIX V
Aircraft Lost on Operations

Date	Pilot	S/N	Origin	Serial	Code	Mark	Fate

Spitfire

05.07.41	Sgt Andrew G. **Costello**	Aus.404086	RAAF	**P8085**		IIA	†

Shot down by an intruder at 01.03 while preparing to land at North Coates aerodrome returning from a night training flight, Somer Coates, Lincs. Australian fresh graduate from Queensland, he was serving the squadron for 10 weeks.

Note on the aircraft: TOC No.38 MU 26.02.41, presentation aircraft 'GARFIELD WESTON VII', issued to No.452 Sqn 27.05.41. Previously served with No.303 (Polish) Sqn.

11.07.41	Sgt Alexander C. **Roberts**	Aus.402007	RAAF	**P7562**		IIA	**Eva.**

Took off at 13.55 for a sweep over France, F/L Finucane was leading the formation. Intercepted by Bf109s and forced to bale out during combat. The rest of the formation returned to base at 15.30. Walked to Calais and the French Resistance helped him to evade via Spain and Gibraltar, returning to the UK three months later and returned to squadron in November. Australian from

New South Wales, he first served with No.607 Sqn between February and April 1941 before joining No.452 Sqn. In April 1942 he was posted to No.258 Sqn and was repatriated in November 1943, having received his commission in January. No more operational postings until the end of war, he was eventually discharged at his own request in June 1945.

Note on the aircraft: TOC No.28 MU 28.10.40, issued to No.452 Sqn 15.06.41. Previously served with Nos.64 and 54 Sqns.

09.08.41   P/O Justin H. **O'Byrne**   Aus.408022   RAAF   **P7682**   IIA   **PoW**

11 aircraft led by the CO took off at 10.35 for CIRCUS *68 to Gosnay. Intercepted around 11.30 between Mardyck and Bethune between 10,000 and 20,000 feet by a Bf109 and shot down, becoming a PoW at Stalag Luft III. Australian from Tasmania he had joined the Squadron in May. It was his first operational posting.*

Note on the aircraft: TOC No.12 MU 22.11.40, issued to No.452 Sqn 27.05.41. Previously served with No.222 Sqn.

Sgt Gerald B. **Haydon**   Aus.404100   RAAF   **P8361**   IIA   †

See above. Australian fresh graduate and native from Queensland, he was among the first pilots to join the squadron in April 1941. Taken prisoner, he died of his wounds a couple of hours later. At 19, he was one of the youngest pilot of the squadron.

Note on the aircraft: TOC No.10 MU 10.04.41, presentation aircraft 'KRAKATAU' issued to No.452 Sqn 04.06.41. Previously served with No.303 (Polish) Sqn.

Sgt Christopher G.B. **Chapman**   Aus.404198   RAAF   **P7590**   IIA   **PoW**

See above. Became a PoW at Stalag 7. Australian from New South Wales, he had joined the squadron in May as his first operational posting. All the remaining aircraft returned to base by 12.40 except Sgt Gazzard who landed at Lympe. The CO's aircraft was lso damaged by cannon fire.

Note on the aircraft: TOC No.12 MU 01.11.40, issued to No.452 Sqn 04.06.41. Previously served with Nos.41 & 303 (Polish) Sqns.

19.08.41   Sgt William D. **Eccleton**   Aus.402232   (NZ)/RAAF   **P8717**   VB   †

A mixed formation of Spitfire II and Vs took of at 10.05 led by the CO for CIRCUS *81 (Gosnay) to form part of the escort. Bounced by Bf109s and posted missing believed killed. His aircraft was seen to lose a wing and spin down out of control. William Eccleton was one of 1,500 New Zealanders who served with the RAAF during WW2 and had joined the squadron in May 41 for his first operational posting.*

Note on the aircraft: TOC No.33 MU 27.07.41, issued to No.452 Sqn 04.08.41.

Sgt Richard G. **Gazzard**   Aus.402115   RAAF   **AB785**   VB   †

See above. Missing. The rest of the formation returned at base by 11.50 but some had to land at Manston or West Malling with the aircraft of Sgt William Willis slightly damaged and aircraft of F/L Douglas' aircraft badly shot up. Australian fresh graduate from New South Wales he had joined the Squadron in April 1941, he was among the first pilots to join the squadron.

Note on the aircraft: TOC No.33 MU 27.07.41, issued to No.452 Sqn 04.08.41.

18.09.41   Sgt Augustine K. **Try**   Aus.402264   RAAF   **W3508**   VB   **PoW**

Twelve Spitfires took off at 14.10 led by the CO for CIRCUS *99 accompanied by Nos.602 and 485 (NZ) Sqn to escort 12 Blenheims to Rouen. The squadron was flying at 10,000 feet crossing the French coast near St-Valery at 14.49 and were engaged by fighters soon after and lost four of their own. Sgt Try is presumed to have been shot down and become a PoW at Stalag Luft IV. Australian from New South Wales he was serving the squadron since three weeks and it was his first operational posting.*

Note on the aircraft: TOC No.37 MU 24.06.41, issued to No.452 Sqn 20.08.41.

Sgt Archibald R. **Stuart**   Aus.402141   RAAF   **P8703**   VB   **PoW**

See above. Became PoW at Stalag Luft 7. Australian fresh graduate and native of New South Wales, was among the first pilots to join the squadron in April 1941.

Note on the aircraft: TOC No.37 MU 18.07.41, issued to No.452 Sqn 11.08.41.

Sgt Charles F.R. **Manning**   Aus.400230   RAAF   **W3600**   VB   †

See above. Killed. Australian from Victoria, he was serving the squadron since end of July. It was his first operational posting.

Note on the aircraft: TOC No.33 MU 14.07.41, issued to No.452 Sqn 24.08.41.

P/O William D. **WILLIS**	Aus.400166	RAAF	**W3512**		VB	†

As above: killed. Australian from Victoria, he had arrived at the squadron early in May. It was his first operational posting. All the rest of the formation had landed to base by 15.50 except Sgt Wawn, P/O Truscott and F/L Douglas who had to refuel at various places before they could rejoin base.

Note on the aircraft: TOC No.12 MU 28.06.41, issued to No.452 Sqn 05.08.41.

20.09.41 Sgt Ian A.L. **MILNE**	Aus.407078	RAAF	**AB841**		VB	**PoW**

Led by S/L Robert Bungey twelve Spitfires took off at 14.10 for CIRCUS 100B accompanied by Nos.602 and 485 (NZ) Sqns to escort Blenheims. On reaching the French Coast a large number of E/A were seen and combat soon engaged. Posted missing from this engagement later reported PoW at Stalag 357. Ian Milne was an Australian from South Australia and had served with No.245 Sqn between February and April 1941 before joining the squadron.

Note on the aircraft: TOC No.45 MU 25.07.41, issued to No.452 Sqn 08.08.41.

12.10.41 Sgt Keith B. **CHISHOLM**	Aus.402150	RAAF	**W3520**		VB	**PoW**

At 11.35, 12 aircraft took off for CIRCUS 107, leading by W/C Ryder. No.452 was forming the lower layer (20,000 feet) escorting 22 Blenheims to the Boulogne docks, crossing the French coast at 12.16. Engaged by E/A and believed to have been shot down and baled out over the sea. Last seen 5/10 miles S East of Le Touquet. All the other returned to the base by 13.25. Native of New South Wales, Australia, Keith Chislolm was picked up by the Germans and later reported PoW. At that time he was credited with 7 confirmed victories (two being shared) with the squadron he had joined in May. A few days later he was awarded the DFM, the first RAAF one in UK. While in the camp, he tried to escape at various times and was eventually successful. He managed to be free in Occupied Europe and was liberated in August 1944 when Paris was liberated.

Note on the aircraft: TOC No.9 MU 27.06.41, issued to No.452 Sqn 11.08.41.

13.10.41 Sgt Edgar P. **JACKSON**	Aus.400227	RAAF	**AB852**		VB	†

At 12.40, twelve aircraft took off led by W/C Ryder for CIRCUS 108, the squadron forming the lower port side of escort to 4 Blenheims whose target was Arques shift-lift. Intercepted by E/A and Sgt Jackson was posted missing presumed shot down. It was his first operational sortie having joined at the end of September. He was native of Victoria, Australia.

Note on the aircraft: TOC No.8 MU 30.07.41, issued to No.452 Sqn 05.08.41.

Sgt John R.H. **ELPHICK**	Aus.402157	RAAF	**AD310**		VB	-

See above. Hit by enemy fighters and forced to bale out over sea and was rescued later in the day. Native of New South Wales, Australia, he had joined the Squadron in August after having served No.111 Sqn between May and August 1941. Repatriated in Australia mid-1942, he left No.452 Sqn and was posted to No.76 Sqn, RAAF with which he served until the beginning 1943. Before the end of the war, he started another tour of operations in March 1945 flying with Nos.113 (ASR) and No.115 (ASR) Flights.

Note on the aircraft: TOC No.8 MU 29.09.41, issued to No.452 Sqn 01.10.41.

06.11.41 Sgt Eric H. **SCHRADER**	Aus.400135	RAAF	**AD242**	UD-E	VB	†

That day the squadron had to work with Kenley Wing (Nos.602 & 485 Sqns) acting as Tomahawk cover, the CO leading the Australians. They took off at 13.45. Engaged by 6 E/A over Cap Gris Nez and Sgt Schrader was posted missing after this combat. Native from Victoria, Australia, Henry Schrader had joined the squadron in August 1941 after having served with No.111 Sqn between May and September 1941.

Note on the aircraft: TOC No.5 MU 13.09.41. Presentation aircraft 'BIHAR IV', issued No.452 Sqn 15.10.41.

Sgt Bernard M. **GEISSMANN**	Aus.404334	RAAF	**AD430**		VB	†

See above. Australian from Queensland, Bernard Geissmann served with No.457 (RAAF) Sqn between June and September 1941 before joining the 452. At 19, he was one os the youngest pilot of the squadron.

Note on the aircraft: TOC No.9 MU 10.10.41, issued to No.452 Sqn 14.41.41.

08.11.41 F/L Keith W. **TRUSCOTT**	Aus.400213	RAAF	**AB842**		VB	-

The squadron took off at 11.00 led by the CO to join Kenley Wing to serve as top cover for Blenheims(CIRCUS 110 – Lille railways workshops). On the way out, while flying at 26,000 feet and about 8 miles inside France, they were attacked by Enemy fighters and 'Bluey' Truscott was hit and was obliged to bale out over the Channel. He was rescued later in the day by an ASR mission. Native of Victoria, Australia, he joined No.452 Sqn direct from OTU in May 1941. Over a year, he proved to be an outstanding pilot in claiming 16 confirmed victories, three being shared, and rose to the head of the Squadron in January 1942. He left the squadron for Australia in March 1942, awarded with the **DFC** & **BAR**. In June, he was posted to No.76 Sqn, RAAF as supernumerary Squadron Leader, and then became the CO of this unit until his death which occurred during a mock attack on a Catalina he was escorting at low altitude. He apparently misjudged his height and flew into the water and was killed in his Kittyhawk A29-150 on 28 March 1943.

Note on the aircraft: TOC No.38 MU 06.07.41. Presentation aircraft 'THE STAFFORDIAN', issued to No.452 Sqn 05.08.41.

| | Sgt Bruce P. **DUNSTAN** | RAF No.1256932 (AUS)/RAF | **P8645** | VB | - |

See above. Rescued with 'Bluey' Truscott. All the remaining aircraft returned to base by 12.50 but Sgt Tainton who landed at Gravesend due to fuel shortage. Bruce Dunstan was an Australian from Victoria who had enlisted in England. It seems that he previously served as recce pilot at No.1 Recce Wing at Babbacombe. He left the squadron the following month and was posted to No.41 Sqn in January 1942 . He was killed in action on 12.02.42 during operation 'Fuller' (Spitfire W3565).

Note on the aircraft: Built as Mk.IIB, presentation aircraft 'FLINT'. TOC No.29 MU 29.04.41, served with No.222 Sqn before being converted to a Mk.VB during summer after damaged sustained in combat on 24.06, and was issued to No.452 Sqn 14.10.41.

| **08.12.41** | Sgt John M. **EMERY** | AUS.407116 | RAAF | **AB966** | VB | † |

Led by the CO the squadron (12 aircraft) took off at 12.30 to act as high cover to rescue a boat off Dungeness. They were later attacked by five Fw190s and Sgt Emery (Black 1) was believed to have been shot down. He was last seen chasing a Fw190 and firing at it towards the French coast. John Emery, an Australian from South Australia, had served with No.457 (RAAF) Sqn between June and August 1941 before being posted to the squadron.

Note on the aircraft: TOC No.37 MU 08.09.41, issued to No.452 Sqn 19.09.41.

| **22.01.42** | P/O Donald E. **LEWIS** | AUS.400148 | RAAF | **AB992** | VB | † |

He took off at 13.55 to lead three other Spitfires for an escort of mine-sweepers, and to join another section led by F/L Thorold-Smith. During the course of this operation, P/O Lewis called up on the RT saying 'I am going into sea', giving his position in the same time. Sgt Harper noticed oil leak on his windscreen. A search was carried out on the course and P/O Lewis was soon found lying on his back in the water his parachute alongside. It was believed that he was unconscious when sighted; F/L Thorold-Smith ordered his section to stand by while he climbed to 3,000 feet to give fixes, but his section mistook his instructions and followed him up. After transmitting long and slow messages, they came down to 100 feet again but could find no trace of P/O Lewis. After orbiting for 40 minutes, the section returned. Australian from Tasmania, he was serving the squadron since May 1941.

Note on the aircraft: TOC No.9 MU 06.10.41, issued to No.452 Sqn 14.10.41. Fitted with a Merlin XX engine.

| **15.02.42** | Sgt Francis G. **HARPER** | AUS.404664 | RAAF | **P8711** | VB | † |

Four aircraft led by P/O Sly took off on scramble at 08.55. They were vectored to an E/A aircraft and attacked it. F/Sgt Makin fired two seconds burst and saw the E/A in difficulty making for the French coast. However Sgt Harper did not return and was last seen following an E/A in a dive. From Queensland, Australia, he was serving the squadron for three months. It was his first operational posting.

Note on the aircraft: TOC No.37 MU 30.07.41, issued to No.452 Sqn 10.08.41.

| **09.03.42** | Sgt Malcolm W. **HAMILTON** | AUS.404726 | RAAF | **AA849** | VB | † |

Led by S/L Truscott, twelve Spitfires took off at 14.25 for a close escort to 6 Bostons (CIRCUS 113), the squadron acting as middle unit for the Kenley Wing, the target being a power station at Marzingarbe. Shortly after having turn left for the way home, about 4 miles West of Lille, the formation was intercepted by Bf109s of the JG26. The squadron was attacked from 200 ft above and astern out of the sun by about 10 Bf109s, later joined by Fw190s. Sgt Hamilton was last seen by P/O Elphick diving down into the water in an inverted position. The last pilots of the squadron landed to base at 16.15. Sgt Hamilton was an Australian from Queensland and had arrived at the Squadron early in November, freshly graduated.

Note on the aircraft: TOC No.38 MU 30.09.41, issued to No.452 Sqn 03.03.42 after served with Nos.54 & 124 Sqns. Buit fitted with a M46 Merlin engine.

| **03.05.42** | P/O John W. **LAMERTON** | AUS.407900 | RAAF | **AD537** | UD-R | VB | - |

P/O Lamerton took off with Sgt Bassett for a defensive patrol at 25,000 feet over Mull of Galloway. While climbing and when at 20,000 feet they saw a Ju88 about 5,000 ft above and the E/A was flying on a S. Easterly course towards the coast. They manoeuvred to get into the sun. P/O Lamberton's attack was from astern and above. He gave a long burst of 3-4 seconds and silenced the top rear gunner using cannon at a range of 300 yards. However P/O Lamerton's aircraft was hit by return fire and flames and smoke came from exhaust and cowling soon appeared. He could see ahead and called up saying that he was baling out, which he did from an altitude of 12,000 feet. He was picked up 6 hours later. Meanwhile Sgt Basset continued to attack the Ju88, but was unable to close to a short range and was recalled to base after he expended all his ammo landing at 07.55. He claimed a damaged aircraft shared with P/O Lamerton. It was the last claim of the squadron while stationed in England. P/O Lamerton was an Australian from South Australia and had joined the squadron three months before from OTU. He was later killed with the squadron [see entry 30.06.43 - Operational losses].

Note on the aircraft: TOC No.37 MU 23.11.41, issued to No.452 Sqn 23.03.42. Previously served with No.457(RAAF)Sqn. FH:124.8

15.03.43   S/L Raymond E. **THOROLD-SMITH**   Aus.402144   RAAF   **BS231**   D   VC/Trop   †

 At 10.30 that day, S/L Thorold-Smith took off on scramble with five other aircraft of the squadron to RAID 53, consisting of 20 bombers and 22 fighters. He was leading the Wing. After the rendezvous with No.54 Sqn, the formation began to climb and upon reaching 20,000 feet they saw the enemy. The idea was to break up the enemy formation before they reached Darwin rather than waiting a real tactical advantage. The Wing attacked without delay but they were bounced by the escorting Japanese fighters. About 30 seconds after the initial attack, a Spitfire was seen smoking and diving vertically near Point Charles, NT which was presumed to be S/L Thorold-Smith's aircraft. At the time of his death, 'Throttle' Thorold-Smith was credited with 7 confirmed victories, one being shared, and had been awarded the DFC in December 1941. His flying abilities were reported as exceptional while in service with No.452 Sqn. [See entry operational losses 11.08.41 and 28.10.41 losses by accident]

Note on the aircraft: TOC (RAF) 28.07.42, to RAAF arrived Melbourne, Australia 14.11.42. Became A58-92 (probably never taken up), issued to No.452 Sqn 03.12.42.

                 F/O Clive P. **LLOYD**   Aus.404690   RAAF   **BS293**   E   VC/Trop   -

See above. F/O Lloyd lost the rest of the formation and attacked three Zekes from front quarter but was himself attacked from behind and eventually hit in the engine. As oil and Glycol leak was covering the wind-screen and smoke was in the cockpit, he decided to dive away from his attackers who did not follow. When conditions became favourable, he abandoned his aircraft at about 5,000 feet 2.5m W of Picnic Point/10m S of Point Charles, unhurt. Australian native of Victoria, he served in the squadron only, between November 1941 and December 1943. [see also operational losses entry 06.07.43].

Note on the aircraft: TOC (RAF) 11.08.42, to RAAF arrived Melbourne, Australia 29.11.42. Became A58-101 (probably never taken up), issued to No.452 Sqn 22.12.42.

02.05.43   F/O Adrian P. **GOLDSMITH**   Aus.402500   RAAF   **BR526**   J   VC/Trop   -

F/O Goldsmith was at readiness that day when the squadron was ordered to scramble RAID 54 launched by the Japanese. T hey took off at 0955, W/C Clive 'Killer' Caldwell flying with the squadron and leading the Wing. An Enemy formation of 21 bombers escorted by 25-30 fighters was sighted at about 27,000 feet approaching Darwin. No.452 Squadron was the last to attack. However, F/O Goldsmith went into attack before the rest of the squadron and was able to penetrate the fighter cover without allowing them to attack him. He was able to make an attack on one bomber and broke away downwards as there were Japanese fighters about to attack him and his aircraft had the controls shot away by a Zero. He was able to evacuate the aircraft which dived into the sea 30m NW of Darwin approximately at 10.45. He was picked up the following day slightly injured. Australian native of New South Wales, 'Tim' Goldsmith had been posted in for a second tour of operations, having served previously in Europe with No.234 Sqn in September 1941 before sailing to Malta in February 1942 where he fought with Nos.242 and 126 Sqns until July 1942. During that time he became one of the most Australian successful pilots of Malta and when he left, he had claimed 13 confirmed victories, one being shared for which he was awarded the DFM and DFC. Serving as instructor for awhile in England, he was repatriated to Australia and joined No.452 Sqn in December 1942. His tour ended in February 1944 and did not fly in operations anymore. He left the service in June 1945, and at that time his score had risen to 17 confirmed victories, one being shared, two probable and seven aircraft damaged, DFM [No.126 Sqn], and DFC [No.126 Sqn].

Note on the aircraft: TOC (RAF) 14.06.42, to RAAF arrived Melbourne, Australia 23.10.42. Became A58-34 (probably never taken up), issued to No.452 Sqn 30.11.42.

                 F/O Alexander C. **McNAB**   Aus.405420   RAAF   **BS225**   B   VC/Trop   †

See above. F/O McNab was flying as White 4 to F/L Hall and was F/O Goldsmith's wingman. In the initial action made by F/O Goldsmith he followed his leader but no one from the Squadron was later able to tell what happened next. It seems that Zero fighters shot away McNab's aircraft controls who baled out 20m W of Perin Islands (appr 10.45). Pilot was rescued but died later. 'Sandy' McNab, an Australian from Queensland, had previously served with No.19 Sqn, RAF in UK for a short time in August-September 1942. He was then repatriated and posted to No.452 Sqn.

Note on the aircraft: TOC (RAF) 02.09.42, to RAAF arrived Melbourne, Australia 24.12.42. Became A58-89 (probably never taken up), issued to No.452 Sqn 31.03.43. Previously served with No.2 OTU.

| P/O Kenneth J. **Fox** | Aus.402330 | RAAF | **BS162** | F | VC/Trop | - |

See above. P/O Fox made three attacks against enemy fighters but was eventually hit in the engine by a fighter attacking from the beam. The engine seized almost at once and the propeller stopped and P/O Fox was forced to abandon the aircraft which ditched into Darwin harbour at approximately 10.45. The pilot was later rescued from his dinghy. Kenneth Fox had joined the squadron in April 1943 for another tour of operations, having completing a previous one with No.124 Sqn in UK between November 1941 and September 1942. In February 1944, his tour expired, and he left the RAAF the following month to serve as a civil pilot in an Australian airways. He was native of New South Wales, Australia.

Note on the aircraft: TOC (RAF) 22.06.42, to RAAF arrived Melbourne, Australia 18.10.42. Became A58-12 (probably never taken up), issued to No.452 Sqn 09.11.42.

| P/O Willie E. **NICHTERLEIN** | Aus.416104 | RAAF | **BS226** | A | VC/Trop | - |

See above. After 15 minutes of combat, P/O Nichterlein, due to shortage of petrol, decided to break away and return to base. However he ran out of fuel and crash-landed in shallows off Tumbling Waters, NT around 11.15. P/O Nichterlein was native from Victoria, Australia, and was serving the squadron since March. He was killed the next month. [see also entry operational losses 20.06.43].

Note on the aircraft: TOC (RAF) 07.09.42, to RAAF arrived Melbourne, Australia 21.11.42. Became A58-90 (probably never taken up), issued to No.452 Sqn 13.03.43. Previously served with No.457 (RAAF) Sqn.

| Sgt Ross S. **STAGG** | Aus.407715 | RAAF | **BR547** | S | VC/Trop | **Inj.** |

See above. Sgt Stagg was flying as Blue 2 to F/L Makin. He followed F/L Makin when he attacked a Zero and F/L Makin broke away climbing steeply to starboard. F/L Makin lost contact with his wingman at that moment. He was later heard on the radio telling that he was bailing out. Failed to return from interception and crashed 10m W of Fog Bay near Darwin, before pilot could bale out. He was later rescued but severely injured and suffering from severe exhaustion and effects of exposure after having wandered through the bush for a fortnight with practically no food. Native of South Australia, Ross Stagg was serving the squadron since April 1942. In July 1944, He returned to the squadron for another tour which ended in March 1945.

Note on the aircraft: TOC (RAF) 20.07.42, to RAAF arrived Melbourne, Australia 23.10.42. Became A58-53 (probably never taken up), issued to No.452 Sqn 09.11.42.

| **20.06.43** | P/O Willie E. **NICHTERLEIN** | Aus.416104 | RAAF | **EE607** | C | VC/Trop | † |

On information received the previous day of an enemy concentration in Timor, the squadron went on readiness at 08.00. At 09.50, news of the enemy's approach was received (RAID No.55) and six Spitfires led by F/L Hall took off five minutes later. A large formation of enemy aircraft were sighted at 24,000 feet. They attacked the Japanese fighters. During the raid the squadron claimed 4 probables and 3 damaged enemy aircraft before they reached their target. However, Willie Nicheterlein failed to return presumed shot down by Zeke fighters and crashed NW of Vernon Island. [see operational losses entry 02.05.43 for details on the pilot].

Note on the aircraft: TOC (RAF) 14.09.42, to RAAF arrived Melbourne, Australia 28.11.42. Became A58-107 (probably never taken up), issued to No.452 Sqn 31.03.43.

| F/Sgt Anthony T. **RUSKIN-ROWE** | Aus.411389 | RAAF | **BS174** | W | VC/Trop | † |

See above. F/Sgt Ruskin-Rowe was flying No.2 to F/O Bisley. Just after a first attack on a bomber led F/O Bisley and the immediate evasive actions which followed it seems that F/Sgt Ruskin was seen alone over Koolpinyah Station, N of Adam Bay, 10m N of Cape Hotham, NT. It is not known if he had been hit by bombers gunners or shot down by Japanese fighters. Sometimes referred as 'Rowe' only, this pilot served at first with No.131 Sqn in England between July and November 1942 and was repatriated to Australia soon after. He was posted to No.24 Sqn, RAAF in February 1943 and joined No.452 Sqn two months later. He was native from New South Wales, Australia.

Note on the aircraft: TOC (RAF) 03.07.42, to RAAF arrived Melbourne, Australia 23.10.42. Became A58-68 (probably never taken up), issued to No.452 Sqn 11.11.42.

| **23.06.43** | F/O Reginald R. **WILLIAMS** | Aus.402675 | RAAF | **AR510** | B | VC/Trop | - |

Led by F/L Evans, six aircraft were scrambled by Fighter sector and took off at 16.55 to investigate an incoming plot. The Liberators were responsible for the investigation. Just out to sea over Point Charles, F/O Williams' aircraft developed Glycol trouble. He tuned back and baled out from 15,000 feet 2 miles East of Point Margaret and 1 mile inland from the south of Tapa Bay, NT. He returned to squadron two days later. Australian native of New South Wales, he had joined the squadron in UK in September 1941, leaving it in October 1943 to never return on operational duty again. He left the RAAF in June 1945 at his own request.

Note on the aircraft: TOC (RAF) 29.06.42, to RAAF arrived Melbourne, Australia 24.12.42. Became A58-1 (probably never taken up), issued to No.452 Sqn 14.05.43. Previously served with No.2 OTU.

28.06.43   F/O Gerald J. **Cowell**   Aus.400967   RAAF   **EE608**   V   VC/Trop   †

That day, F/O Cowell took off for a scramble at 10.30, flying as 'Blue 4' to F/L Evans. After making rendezvous with the Wing, they began to climb North to Cape Gambier. At approximately 18,000 feet, F/O Cowell noticed Glycol smoke streaming from his starboard exhaust indicating a Glycol leak. He then broke the formation after having reported this fact over the radio and began preparations for a forced landing which he did wheels up, on the beach between Gun Point and Tree Point. Gerald Cowell was native of Victoria, Australia and had previously served with No.123 Sqn in UK between January and April 1942, before being posted to No.54 Sqn with which he left for Australia. He left it in November 1942 at the end of his tour. He started another tour with the squadron in March 1943 he completed in December and never flew again in operations.

Note on the aircraft: TOC (RAF) 15.09.42, to RAAF arrived Melbourne, Australia 21.11.42. Became A58-108 (probably never taken up), issued to No.452 Sqn 24.02.43.

30.06.43   F/Sgt Colin R. **Duncan**   Aus.401778   RAAF   **AR523**   A   VC/Trop   -

Led by the CO, S/L MacDonald, twelve Spitfires took off on scramble at 11.25 to intercept the RAID 57 to Darwin, joining Nos.54 and 457 Sqns. They soon reach 28,000 feet and the Wing and the 452 were the last to engage and Blue section the last one of the squadron to engage too. His engine caught fire during engagement and forced to bale out in rough country 18m SW of Batchelor. He was rescued by a rescued party four days later. Australian from Victoria, during the war he served only with No.452 Sqn, between March 1943 and January 1944.

Note on the aircraft: TOC (RAF) 13.07.42, to RAAF arrived Melbourne, Australia 24.12.42. Became A58-2 (probably never taken up), issued to No.452 Sqn 14.05.43. Previously served with No.2 OTU & No.24 Sqn, RAAF.

           F/O William J. **Lamerton**   Aus.407900   RAAF   **BR241**   T   VC/Trop   †

See above, acting as 'Red 4'. Crashed about a quarter of mile beyond the north end of the strip. He had been obliged to turn back from our intercepting force owing to Glycol trouble while flying at 16,000 feet. He attempted to force-land but overshot the strip and the wheels touched down at considerable speed causing the aircraft to bounce and eventually crashed in the cleared approached way. The aircraft exploded five seconds after it had settled leaving no time to escape. He was however rapidly extracted alive but with 3rd degree burns and was rushed to hospital. He died later in the evening. He was serving the squadron since October 1941 and was native of South Australia.

Note on the aircraft: TOC (RAF) 04.07.42, to RAAF arrived Melbourne, Australia 23.10.42. Became A58-19 (probably never taken up), issued to No.452 Sqn 09.11.42.

           F/Sgt Keith S. **Cross**   Aus.403130   RAAF   **BR546**   S   VC/Trop   -

See above. Developed engine trouble (over-revved) while about to engage the Enemy and made a wheels-up force-landing on Batchelor-Stapleton road, 15m NW of Batchelor. Pilot was slightly injured. Cross was serving the squadron since Spring 1942 at Isle of Man and after recovery completed his tour in October. He also served briefly as instructor in 1941. Saw no more action until the end of the war. He was native of New South Wales, Australia and remained with the RAAF after the war.

Note on the aircraft: TOC (RAF) 15.07.42, to RAAF arrived Melbourne, Australia 23.10.42. Became A58-52 (probably never taken up), issued to No.452 Sqn 27.11.42.

06.07.43   F/O Clive P. **Lloyd**   Aus.404690   RAAF   **BR497**   QY-C   VC/Trop   -

Ten squadron aircraft took off at 10.40 to took part of an interception force (RAID 58) with Nos.54 and 457 Sqns against an enemy formation to attack Fenton, S/L MacDonald leading. F/O Lloyd was acting as White 3 behind F/L E.S. Hall. During the dogfight he and Sgt Richardson were attack by three Zeros. F/O Llyod broke to the right and dived with Zekes following for some time before spinning but the engine was eventually hit and caught fire at 10,000 feet obliging the pilot to abandon the aircraft. He parachuted safely while his Spitfire crashed in Coomalie Creek area, 15m W of Strauss. The remaining aircraft landed at base by 12.30. F/O Lloyd had already had to abandon his aircraft the previous March. [see entry 15.03.43 regarding details on the pilot].

Note on the aircraft: TOC (RAF) 14.06.42, to RAAF arrived Melbourne, Australia 18.10.42. Became A58-32 (probably never taken up), issued to No.452 Sqn 09.11.42.

           Sgt Arthur R. **Richardson**   Aus.411644   RAAF   **BR237**   VC/Trop   -

See above. Attacked by three Zekes, he attempted to break down and away but was hit. His cockpit was enveloped with smoke and fire and abandoned the aircraft at 27,000 feet. Arthur Richardson, Australian native of New South Wales, had joined the squadron in April 1943, but had served with No.167 Sqn in UK between September 1942 and February 1943. He continued to fly with the squadron until the end of his tour in February 1944.

Note on the aircraft: TOC (RAF) 22.06.42, to RAAF arrived Melbourne, Australia 23.10.42. Became A58-15 (probably never taken up), issued to No.452 Sqn 26.11.42.

F/L Paul St-J. **Makin**		RAF No.116507	(AUS)/RAF	**BS193**	VC/Trop	-

See above. Engine failed during engagement and pilot baled out safely 30m N of Fenton. Native of South Australia, Paul Makin enlisted in England in the RAF, and served briefly with No.245 Sqn before being posted to No.452 Sqn in April 1941. He left the squadron in July 1943 at the end of his tour. He survived the war and remained with the RAF after the war, but transferred to the RAAF later on.
Note on the aircraft: TOC (RAF) 27.07.42, to RAAF arrived Melbourne, Australia 14.11.42. Became A58-79 (probably never taken up), issued to No.452 Sqn 15.12.42.

07.09.43	S/L Ronald S. **MacDonald**	Aus.270812	RAAF	**A58-227** QY-D	VC/Trop	-

Scrambled at 09.25 to lead the Squadron to intercept an armed escorted reconnaissance formation, being 'Red 1' in the formation. At 23,000 feet 15 miles from Strauss they were attacked by about 16 Japanese fighters. Hit by Enemy aircraft and forced to bale out injured 15mW of Strauss, one shell having exploded in his cockpit and suffering severe burns. Enlisted in the Citizen Air Force, S/L MacDonald native of Queensland, Australia, had served with No.25 Sqn, RAAF between October 1940 and April 1942, then No.12 Sqn, RAAF until March 1943 when he joined No.452 Sqn. He left the squadron at the end of his tour in February 1944.
Note on the aircraft: TOC (RAF) 02.05.43 as LZ884, to RAAF arrived Melbourne, Australia 30.06.43. Issued to No.452 Sqn 09.08.43.

	P/O Paul D. **Tully**	Aus.404998	RAAF	**A58-55** QY-K	VC/Trop	-

See above, acting as 'Red 2'. Hit behind the cockpit and in the engine and baled out. Paul Tully was closed to complete his tour with the squadron as he was flying with it since April 1942. He left in October 1943 and never flew in operations again. He was native of Queensland, Australia. [see also losses by accident 21.02.43].
Note on the aircraft: TOC (RAF) 24.07.42 as BR549, to RAAF arrived Melbourne, Australia 23.10.42. Issued to No.452 Sqn 09.11.42.

12.06.44	F/O Colin H. **O'Laughlin**	Aus.407449	RAAF	**A58-117**	VC/Trop	-

F/O O'Laughlin was Yellow 4 and No.2 to P/O M.J. Beaton took off at 07.00 to intercept a Dinah and contact was made over Point Blaze at 08.09 which was shot down. In the climb, the engine began to give some trouble but the pilot decided to continue the operations by staying at 28,000 feet and not trying to go higher. They sighted the Dinah and proceeded to attack. During the attack the engine of F/O O'Laughlin's aircraft over-revved forcing him to abandon at 13,000 feet 5 m S of Point Blaze. He landed in the sea close to the shore. He stayed afloat until he was picked up by a Catalina of No.43 Sqn two hours later. O'Laughlin, a South Australian, had joined the squadron in October 1943 and completed his tour in September 1944. It was his first operational posting.
Note on the aircraft: TOC (RAF) 27.10.42 as EE673, to RAAF arrived Melbourne, Australia 28.02.43. Issued to No.452 Sqn 10.07.43 and then again on 04.04.44 after a short stay at No.54 Sqn, RAF between 03.01.44 and 04.04.44.

24.12.44	F/O Ian A. **Markwell**	Aus.414054	RAAF	**A58-519**	LF.VIIIC	†

While flying on an offensive patrol over Halmaheras led by W/C Caldwell, the engine stopped about 10 minutes after take off, flying at 4,500 feet. The pilot left formation and he tried to restart the engine without success. He was obliged to evacuate the Spitfire when about 2,000 feet over the sea off Morotai. An ASR mission was launched and located the parachute but not the pilot. Markwell began in Europe with No.132 Sqn with which he completed a full tour between December 1942 and November 1943 and was then repatriated. He had joined the squadron the previous September for a second tour. He was native of Queensland, Australia.
Note on the aircraft: TOC (RAF) 28.04.44 as MT620, to RAAF arrived Melbourne, Australia 15.07.44. Issued to No.452 Sqn 14.12.44.

28.12.44	F/O Alan J. **Proctor**	Aus.418174	RAAF	**A58-400**	LF.VIIIC	-

On take-off prior to carrying out a night patrol, the aircraft swung to the left. The aircraft climbed the left-hand embankment and skidded completely around causing major damages, pilot escaping injuries. Native of Victoria, Australia, Proctor served as flying instructor for many months before joining the squadron in July 1944 for his first operational assignment. He was about to completed his tour in July 1945 when he was killed in action on 2nd July.
Note on the aircraft: TOC (RAF) 24.11.43 as MD223, to RAAF arrived Sydney, Australia 29.02.44. Issued to No.452 Sqn 28.12.44, served previously with No.457(RAAF)Sqn.

07.01.45	P/O Hugh S. **McNeil**	Aus.432834	RAAF	**A58-440**	LF.VIIIC	**Inj.**

P/O MacNeil took off at 17.55 as No.2 of F/O RS Stagg for an intruder mission over the Halmaheras. Hit by ground fire just behind the pilot's seat. It is presumed that a bullet also hit the Glycol system as the temperature rose rapidly and the engine seized in flight. The pilot was able to re-start the engine and tried to make a safe way home but failed and crashed at 18.36 in a heavy timber on Cape Gela (Morotai), some 3m from Pitoe Strip. P/O MacNeil was severely injured in the head and could not escape alone. He was extracted by an American officer before the flames could burn him. Hugh McNeil was native of New South Wales, Australia, and was serving the squadron since May 1944.

Note on the aircraft: TOC (RAF) 12.03.44 as JG665, to RAAF arrived Sydney, Australia 19.06.44. Issued to No.452 Sqn 13.12.44.

13.01.45   F/O Albert L. **LUMLEY**   Aus.411587   RAAF   **A58-466**   LF.VIIIC   -

Took off at 01.50 as No.1 with F/O Logan and F/O Stagg for a standing patrol over Morotai. As the aircraft gathered speed the tail began to rise on take-off, the pilot's attention was distracted by a bright flash of light on the starboard side. The pilot was disconcerted by the light in the belief that a motor vehicle was on the edge of the strip and swung to port and crashed, suffering slight injuries. Australian native of New South Wales, he first served with No.131 Sqn in UK between September 1942 and July 1943 before being repatriated to Australia where he was posted to No.457 (RAAF) Sqn in May 1944 for another tour. In December he was posted to No.452 Sqn and left one week after the accident.

Note on the aircraft: TOC (RAF) 04.02.44 as MD252, to RAAF arrived Sydney, Australia 09.05.44. Issued to No.452 Sqn 10.12.44, served previously with No.457(RAAF)Sqn.

             F/Sgt Edmond MacL. **STEVENSON**   Aus.432589   RAAF   **A58-419**   LF.VIIIC   **PoW**

Led by F/O Proctor, four aircraft took off at 15.35 for an intruder patrol. A barge was seen and attacked and F/Sgt Stevenson flying as No.2 of W/O Byrne, disappeared suddenly over Ternate Island while they were flying at 5,000 feet. F/Sgt Stevenson's radio-transmitter was unserviceable at the time, so no one could learn what had happened. His Spitfire was soon found by W/O Byrne off shore in the shallow water with the tail visible, but no sign of Stevenson. Later reported as a PoW where he was reported to have died on 14.04.45. Native of New South Wales, Australia, he was serving the squadron since February 1944 and was close to finish his tour.

Note on the aircraft: TOC (RAF) 24.12.43 as JG543, to RAAF arrived Brisbane, Australia 07.04.44. Issued to No.452 Sqn 10.12.44, served previously with No.457(RAAF)Sqn.

18.01.45   F/L Leslie A. **LEEMING**   Aus.400992   RAAF   **A58-524**   LF.VIIIC   †

Took off at 20.10 as No.2 to S/L Birch for a standing night patrol. Suffered an engine failure around 21.00 and in attempting to land he stuck a bank of earth some distance short of the runway and crashed killing him instantly. Leslie Leeming was serving the squadron for about a month, but he began his military pilot career as flying instructor before he joined No.457 (RAAF) Sqn in May 1944 as first operational assignment. He was an Australian native of Victoria.

Note on the aircraft: TOC (RAF) 22.05.44 as MT549, to RAAF arrived Sydney, Australia 27.07.44. Issued to No.452 Sqn 10.12.44.

02.07.45   F/O Alan J. **PROCTOR**   Aus.418174   RAAF   **A58-465**   QY-K   LF.VIIIC   †

At 14.25, S/L Barclay took off for a strike against Semaloemoeng leading three other aircraft. Two direct hits with bombs were recorded on a large hut. F/L Proctor failed to return from this sortie and his Spitfire was seen burning on the ground near the target, N of Tarakan Is off NE Borneo. [See entry 28.12.44 of the operational losses for details on the pilot].

Note on the aircraft: TOC (RAF) 28.01.44 as MT545, to RAAF arrived Melbourne, Australia 19.05.44. Issued to No.452 Sqn 04.05.45. Served previously with No.457(RAAF)Sqn.

07.07.45   F/Sgt Brian F. **GURNEY**   Aus.439285   RAAF   **A58-458**   LF.VIIIC   -

Owing to bad weather, four aircraft en route for another target, the second of the day had to return after 45 minutes of flight. F/Sgt Gurney whose air speed indicator had become unserviceable, misjudged his path and approached too fast. Bounced on landing and took off again but in the following circuit, the starboard undercarriage leg remained retracted. He continued the landing with a jammed main leg, hit bank, Pitoe, Morotai. Although the pilot was uninjured, the aircraft was a total write-off. Native of New South Wales, Australia, Brian Gurney was serving the Squadron since November 1944, but flew temporary with No.457 (RAAF) Sqn between December 1944 and February 1945. He served the squadron until the end. (see also operational losses entry 17.07.45).

Note on the aircraft: TOC (RAF) 28.01.44 as MD297, to RAAF arrived Melbourne, Australia 19.05.44. Issued to No.452 Sqn 10.12.44. Served previoulsy with No.457(RAAF)Sqn.

10.07.45   F/L Norman J. **CULLEN**   Aus.406070   RAAF   **A58-518**   QY-O   LF.VIIIC   †

Four aircraft took off at 11.35 to attack Japanese bridges and troop concentrations in Tawao area (NE of Borneo), the CO leading. The bridges were attack using dive bombing techniques and near misses were recorded damaging a bridge and a W/T installation which was set on fire by strafing. F/L Cullen failed to return, and was last seen recovering from his dive bombing run. Although an immediate search was carried out by the three other aircraft, no wreckage was located and they resumed their flight back to base where they landed at 13.25. In the afternoon, two Spitfires were sent with Kittyhawks to conduct further search but with no positive results. Native of Western Australia, Cullen had completed a tour with No.127 Sqn in North Africa and the Mediterranean before being repatriated. He joined the squadron for another tour in November 1944, but served also for a couple of days with No.457 (RAAF) Sqn in December 1944.

Note on the aircraft: TOC (RAF) 23.04.44 as MT618, to RAAF arrived Melbourne, Australia 15.07.44. Issued to No.452 Sqn 10.12.44.

12.07.45	S/L Kevin M. **BARCLAY**	Aus.407662	RAAF	**A58-647**	HF.VIIIC	-

S/L Barclay took off at 11.15 leading three others Spitfires of the squadron to dive bomb bridges from 3,000 feet and to strafe huts over Morotai River again in Tawor area. Hit by ack-ack during his dive bombing run, he was force to abandon his aircraft which crashed in the sea off the coast, while he landed in the water midway between Sebatik and Boekay Islands. He was rescued from his dinghy three hours later. Kevin Barclay was only Australian to have served in three Australian squadrons raised under Article XV regulations. Indeed, after having briefly served Nos.32 and 66 Sqns in England between October 1941 and January 1942 he was posted in November 1942 to No.453 (RAAF) Sqn based in UK and was called to lead the unit in May 1943 until the end of his tour in September, leaving awarded with a DFC. He was repatriated in Australia in May 1944 and the following month he was posted to No.457 (RAAF) Sqn as supernumerary Squadron Leader for the year to come. In June 1945, he joined No.452 Sqn as CO until 12 September. He served the RAAF after the war and was native of South Australia.

Note on the aircraft: TOC (RAF) 18.09.44 as MV476, to RAAF arriving Sydney, Australia 30.11.44. Issued to No.452 Sqn 02.07.45.

17.07.45	F/Sgt Brian F. **GURNEY**	Aus.439285	RAAF	**A58-516**	QY-E	LF.VIIIC	-

At 11.50 five Spitfires took off to strafe enemy troops in Balikpapan area. The formation was led by S/L Barclay. On landing around 12.05 F/Sgt Gurney misjudged his landing and touched down short of the firm runway. The soft mud caused the plane to nose over, cartwheel and burst into flame. The pilot escaped with a shaking up. Due to the fire tender's foam extinguisher running out the aircraft burned back to the cockpit. It was his second misadventure since the beginning of the month. [see also operational losses entry 07.07.45 for details on the pilot].

Note on the aircraft: TOC (RAF) 06.04.44 as JG690, to RAAF arrived Sydney, Australia 17.07.44. Issued to No.452 Sqn 10.12.44. Damaged in an accident on 12.04.45, it returned at the squadron on 15.06.45.

04.08.45	F/O Edmund H. **LEE**	Aus.419722	RAAF	**A58-650**	HF.VIIIC	†

Whilst on take-off on a scramble for a lost Kittyhawk, collided with a truck parked on edge of the runway just after becoming airborne at Croydon Strip, Tarakan. He died from injuries 11 days later on the 15th the day of the Japanese surrender. Lee, native of Victoria, Australia had previously served as flying instructor before joining No.452 Sqn at the end of June 1945, as being his first operational posting.

Note on the aircraft: TOC (RAF) 25.09.44 as MV479, to RAAF arrived Sydney, Australia 30.11.44. Issued to No.452 Sqn 28.07.45.

Total: 56

APPENDIX VI
AIRCRAFT LOST IN ACCIDENTS

Date	Pilot	S/N	Origin	Serial	Code	Mark	Fate

SPITFIRE

03.05.41	S/L Roy G. **DUTTON**	RAF No.39072	RAF	**X4825**	IA	-

That day, the squadron carried out an air drill-over between Scunthorpe, Lics, and Brighouse, Yorks, in connection with the two town's "War Weapon week". Near Halifax, when flying in close formation over very broken country, the airscrew of Finucane's aircraft came into contact with the empennage of S/L Duttun's aircraft, partially severing the structure. Although the CO had no force and aft control over his aircraft, he was able by the use of the engine and severe pulls on his control columns to keep the aircraft from losing height too steeply. At the same time he turned to port thereby gaining the open country and crashed going through a stone wall. The CO was slightly injured but returned later to the squadron the same day while F/L 'Paddy' Finucane was able to land. Roy Dutton was a pre-war RAF pilot and was serving with No.111 Sqn when the war broke out before being posted to No.145 Sqn in April 1940 with which he fought during the Battle of Britain. A couple of weeks after the accident, Roy Dutton left the squadron to take command No.19 Sqn at Fowlmere for about a month. In March 1942, he returned to a front-line unit for another tour, a night fighter unit, No.141 Sqn flying Beaufighters. At the end of November 1942, he left No.141 Sqn to take various HQ appointment. In 1945, he became CO of a transport squadron, Nos.512. He remained with the RAF after the War, retiring as an Air Commodore in 1970. In all he was credited with 19 confirmed victories, 6 being shared with Nos.111, 145 and 19 Sqns, DSO [No.525 Sqn], DFC & BAR [both No.145 Sqn].

Note on the aircraft: TOC No.9 MU 05.12.40, issued to No.452 Sqn 19.04.41.

11.06.41   P/O Raymond E. THOROLD-SMITH   Aus.402144   RAAF   **P8130**   IIA   -
Crashed on take-off from Sutton Bridge for an Air-firing exercise. 'Throttle' Thorold-Smith was an Australian from New South Wales. Later killed in action over Darwin. [See entry Operational losses 15.03.43, but also entry 28.10.41, accident below]

Note on the aircraft: TOC No.8 MU 06.04.41, presentation aircraft 'LUTON I' issued to No.452 Sqn 04.06.41. Served previously with No.303 (Polish) Sqn.

07.09.41   Sgt Kenneth V. WILLIAMS   Aus.400264   RAAF   **P8716**   VB   †
Collided with Sgt J.N. Hannigan's aircraft when doing dummy attacks and crashed. Australian from Victoria, he had served briefly with No.457 (RAAF) Sqn between June and August 1941 before joining No.452 Sqn.

Note on the aircraft: TOC No.33 MU 27.07.41, issued to No.452 Sqn 04.08.41.

          Sgt John N. HANNIGAN   Aus.402120   RAAF   **AB874**   VB   †
Collided with Sgt KennethWilliam's aircraft when doing dummy attacks and crashed. John Neate Hannigan was native from New South Wales, Australia, and was serving with the Squadron for five months. It was his first operational posting.

Note on the aircraft: TOC No.37 MU 09.08.41, issued to No.452 Sqn 18.08.41.

28.10.41   F/L Raymond E. THOROLD-SMITH   Aus.402144   RAAF   **W3821**   UD-D   VB   -
F/L Thorold-Smith took off before mid-day for a Balbo exercise leading 11 others aircraft. On return at Redhill at 12.50, a tyre burst on landing and the aircraft ground looped and tipped up. Aircraft was not repaired and was SOC later. 'Throttle' Thorold-Smith was an Australian from New South Wales. Later killed in action over Darwin. [See entry Operational losses 15.03.43, but also entry 11.06.41, accident above]

Note on the aircraft: TOC No.9 MU 27.08.41, presentation aircraft 'PEMBA III', issued to No.452 Sqn 11.09.41.

04.01.42   P/O Allenby L. BAKER   Aus.403159   RAAF   **AB195**   VB   †
During a cannon test, the Spitfire was seen by witnesses ditching ½ m SW of Beachy Head, Sussex, cause not known. Pilot native of New South Wales, Australia, he had arrived at the squadron less than two weeks before as his first operational posting.

Note on the aircraft: TOC No.12 MU 12.12.41, issued to No.452 Sqn 28.12.41.

10.04.42   Sgt Ralph E. WATERS   Aus.408165   RAAF   **BL384**   VB   †
During a squadron formation practice from Base to St-Bee's Head, Sgt Waters was first seen lagging in formation. After the squadron had been given the order to break and had reformed again it was observed that Sgt Waters was nowhere to be seen, and did not return to base as many were thinking he had done. Later the Coast Guards confirmed that a Spitfre had been seen crashing into the sea about 8 miles SW of St-Bees Head. However not trace could be found of either his body or aircraft. Ralph Waters was native of Victoria, Australia, and had just joined the squadron.

Note on the aircraft: TOC No.12 MU 27.11.41, issued to No.452 Sqn 23.03.42. Previously served with No.457(RAAF)Sqn.

07.05.42   P/O Robert H. WHILLANS   Aus.404693   RAAF   **AB171**   VB   -
At 18.00 P/O Whillans took off with F/L Makin to do some practice cloud flying. P/O Whillans' aircraft developed an internal glycol leak, and as smoke and fumes filled the cockpit controls failed to respond forcing him to bale out which he did successfully 1 mile East of Jurby aerodrome. Australia from Queensland, Australia, he had joined the Squadron in November 1941 as his first opera-

tional posting. He left the squadron at the end of his tour in December 1943 and never flew again in operations.
Note on the aircraft: TOC No.39 MU 23.11.41, issued to No.452 Sqn 23.03.42. Previously served with No.457(RAAF)Sqn.

08.05.42   P/O William H. **FORD**   Aus.401429   RAAF   **AB244**   VB   -
When practising camera quarter attacks, P/O Ford being the target, Sgt Goodhew by an error of judgement made a head-on attack and failed to break away and collided. P/O Ford was able to bale out however. Australian from Victoria, he had joined the squadron in March. Later killed while serving the squadron [see entry 27.02.43 - losses by accident].
Note on the aircraft: TOC No.8 MU 30.11.41, issued to No.452 Sqn 23.03.42. Previously served with No.457(RAAF)Sqn.

                  Sgt Regilnald A. **GOODHEW**   Aus.403332   RAAF   **BL351**   UD-H   VB   †
See above. Killed. He had joined the Squadron at the end of March and was native of New South Wales, Australia.
Note on the aircraft: TOC No.9 MU 24.11.41, issued to No.452 Sqn 23.03.42. Previously served with No.457(RAAF)Sqn.

09.10.42   Sgt Michael **CLIFFORD**   Aus.403320   RAAF   **BR471**   VC/Trop   †
Dived into sea 1m off shore near Wamberal. This accident occurred during an authorised flight in the aim to carry out an oxygen climb to 35,000 feet. His body was washed up on the beach the following day. Native of New South Wales, Australia, he was serving the squadron since May.
Note on the aircraft: TOC (RAF) 21.05.42, to RAAF arrived Australia 25.08.42. Became A58-25 (probably never taken up), issued to No.452 Sqn 05.10.42.

17.12.42   F/O Robert **ARMSTRONG**   Aus.403463   RAAF   **BS230**   VC/Trop   **Inj.**
Starboard leg collapsed and gave way on landing after a training flight. The aircraft shot over on its nose and overturned. F/O Armstrong was trapped in the aircraft and was extracted with difficulties and was injured. He was taken to the hospital with a knee dislocated. Australian from New South Wales, he had joined the squadron one year before. It was his operational posting.
Note on the aircraft: TOC (RAF) 26.07.42, to RAAF arrived Melbourne, Australia 23.10.42. Became A58-91 (probably never taken up), issued to No.452 Sqn 11.11.42.

27.01.43   Sgt Eric E. **HUTCHINSON**   Aus.403602   RAAF   **BS184**   VC/Trop   †
Mid-air collision with Spitfire BR549 flown by Sgt Stockley during exercise making a dummy attack on a Liberator. In the break the two aircraft made a converging attack. Sgt Hutchinson flying at a faster speed than Sgt Stockley and his tail hit the port wing of Sgt Stocley's aircraft. Sgt Hutchinson's aircraft plunged to the ground and he had no opportunity to bale out, while Sgt Stockey was able to make a safe landing with a buckled port wing. Sgt Hutchison crashed 4m SE of Coomalie Creek, NT. Eric Hutchinson had joined the squadron the previous month but had served before in UK with No.234 Sqn between April and August 1942. He was native of New South Wales, Australia.
Note on the aircraft: TOC (RAF) 13.07.42, to RAAF arrived Melbourne, Australia 23.10.42. Became A58-73 (probably never taken up), issued to No.452 Sqn 14.11.42.

17.02.43   F/O John G. **GOULD**   Aus.404613   RAAF   **BR584**   VC/Trop   -
The squadron was carrying out night flying practice from Batchelor and F/O Gould was authorised doing circuits and landings. Misjudged distance on landing and made an undershot landing at night about 400 yards of the runway, hit tree and crashed at Strauss strip at about 21.25. John Gould, an Australian from Queensland had joined the squadron for the first time March 1942 posted from No.275 Sqn with which he was flying since October 1941. He previously served with No.457 (RAAF) Sqn in September-October 1941. He returned for a very short time with No.457 (RAAF) Sqn in April 1942 before returning to No.452 Sqn until the end of his tour in November 1943. It was his last operational posting for the war.
Note on the aircraft: TOC (RAF) 01.06.42, to RAAF arrived Melbourne, Australia 23.10.42. Became A58-60 (probably never taken up), issued to No.452 Sqn 05.12.42.

21.02.43   Sgt Paul D. **TULLY**   Aus.404998   RAAF   **BR386**   K   VC/Trop   -
At about 11.00, while on an authorised height and engine test flight, engine cut at 28,000'; he glided down but at 600' he

ran into a cloud, turned too far to port and eventually crashed at right angles to the strip at about 20 yards east of the centre of Strauss strip. Sgt Tully was slight injured. (See operational losses 07.09.43 for details on the pilot).
Note on the aircraft: TOC (RAF) 10.05.42, to RAAF arrived Australia 25.08.42. Became A58-22 (probably never taken up), issued to No.452 Sqn 28.09.42.

27.02.43   F/O William H. **FORD**   Aus.401429   RAAF   **BS175**   VC/Trop   †
One flight of six aircraft took off from Wyndham at 16.30 to operate from there temporarily. The formation was led by F/L Hall and was accompanied by a Hudson which was serving as navigator and transporting equipment and servicing party. The formation encountered bad weather with 10/10 clouds at 1,000 feet, followed by a thunderstorm reducing visibility to a few yards only. When the formation flew out of the thunderstorm, WH Ford was absent and he never reached the destination. The wreckage was later found on 6th March crashed at Tabletop Range. William Ford, an Australian from Victoria, was serving the squadron since June 1942.
Note on the aircraft: TOC (RAF) 06.07.42, to RAAF arrived Melbourne, Australia 23.10.42. Became A58-69 (probably never taken up), issued to No.452 Sqn 15.11.42.

06.03.43   Sgt Eric M. **MOORE**   Aus.403357   RAAF   **BS237**   K   VC/Trop   †
When on aircraft test, Spitfire BS237 developed a glycol leak when at 28,000'. He came down with F/O Williams attempting to lead him into Strauss. He came down to 1,000' to get below cloud base (there was a ceiling 10/10), and said he was going to bail out but crashed 5-6 miles from the aerodrome with nose well forward. Eric Moore, Australian native of New South Wales, was serving the squadron for one year.
Note on the aircraft: TOC (RAF) 20.08.42, to RAAF arrived Melbourne, Australia 02.12.42. Became A58-98 (probably never taken up), issued to No.452 Sqn 24.02.43.

22.03.43   Sgt William M. **COOMBES**   Aus.403800   RAAF   **BS163**   B   VC/Trop   -
That day, Sgt Coombes was authorised to carry out formation practice in a section of three. On return Sgt Coombes was the last to land at 18.23. When he had run well down the runway, the aircraft developed a slight swing to the left towards the trees. He tried to correct this in acting in the opposite direction, but the aircraft swung to the right this time, a swing which he was unable to counter. The aircraft ran across the road alongside the runway and caught the undercarriage on the pipe line. The tail lifted and flopped back again. Australian native of New South Wales, he began his operational career with No.41 Sqn, RAF in England between June and September 1942 before being repatriated in Australia. He joined the squadron in March 1943 and completed his tour in February 1944. He returned to the squadron for another tour in August 1945. He remained with the RAAF after the war retiring a Wing Commander in 1968. [See also losses by accident 30.08.45]
Note on the aircraft: TOC (RAF) 22.06.42, to RAAF arrived Melbourne, Australia 18.10.42. Became A58-12 (probably never taken up), issued to No.452 Sqn 09.11.42.

05.08.43   F/O John H.E. **BISLEY**   Aus.402720   RAAF   **A58-6**   QY-R   VC/Trop   -
F/O Bisley was leading a practice formation when at 8,000 feet he developed a Glycol leak obliging him to crash-land hitting an anthill W. of Middle Arm, Darwin. Bisley of New South Wales, Australia, had joined the squadron in November 1942 after having served in Europe with No.122 Sqn, (September 1941 – March 1942), in Malta with No.126 Sqn (March – July 1942) with which he shot down 6 confirmed aircraft, one being shared, and was awarded the DFC. He had claimed another and last victory on the 20th June. He left the squadron in January 1944 and never saw action again, leaving the RAAF in August 1945.
Note on the aircraft: TOC (RAF) 27.07.42 as AR563, to RAAF arrived Melbourne, Australia 29.11.42 Issued to No.452 Sqn 14.05.42. Previously served with No.2 OTU and No.24 Sqn, RAAF.

26.09.43   F/O Granville A. **MAWER**   Aus.403112   RAAF   **A58-201**   VC/Trop   †
That day, F/O Mawer was authorised to do an aircraft test and a camera gun attack on White section of four aircraft. In the vicinity of Manton Dam, F/O Mawer contacted White section and proceeded to attack them. After his first attack he passed under the Section and was followed by F/L Goldsmith. F/O Adam then came in to 'attack' him from the above then broke upwards and to starboard. Mawer, not knowing where F/O Adam was at this stage, proceeded to pull his aircraft into a steep climbing turn also to starboard. The port wings of both aircraft collided, breaking off at approximately the inboard end of the aileron. Both aircraft immediately spun into the ground killing both pilots. Granville Mawer had joined the squadron in March and was native of New South Wales, Australia.
Note on the aircraft: TOC (RAF) 31.05.43 as JL314, to RAAF arrived Australia 02.08.43. Issued to No.452 Sqn 15.09.43.

P/O John P. **ADAM**	Aus.404491	RAAF	**A58-121**		VC/Trop	†

See above. Native of New South Wales, Australia, 'Phil' Adam as he was known from his second christian name, served at first with No.457 (RAAF) Sqn for one month in Autumn 1941, before being posted to No.275 Sqn when it was formed in October 1941, flying Lysanders and Walruses until May 1942 when he joined the squadron.

Note on the aircraft: TOC (RAF) 27.10.42 as EE677, to RAAF arrived Melbourne, Australia 22.02.43. Issued to No.452 Sqn 16.07.43.

10.12.43	F/O Frederick R. **MCCANN**	Aus.402129	RAAF	**A58-205**	QY-Y	VC/Trop	-

At approximately 09.30, F/O McCann was returning to base from training flying, when he discovered that the Air Speed Indicator had stuck at 260 mph. He then arranged for F/Sgt Richardson to lead him into the landing. F/O McCann made a normal landing and ran some distance then the port tyre burst causing the aircraft to swing to port. Despite pilot's efforts to correct the swing, the aircraft ran off the strip, and the port leg collapsed. The pilot escaped injuries. Native of Tasmania, Australia, it was actually the second time he was serving the squadron. Indeed, he served with it in England between May and December 1941 (which includes a short stay with No.72 Sqn in July 1941). In October 1942 he was posted to No.453 (RAAF) Sqn based in UK, he left in June 1943 to be repatriated to Australia. He returned to the squadron in November 1943 and flew with it until June 1944. It was his last operational posting.

Note on the aircraft: TOC (RAF) 19.04.43 as JL378, to RAAF arrived Australia 03.07.43. Issued to No.452 Sqn 09.08.43.

11.12.43	P/O Jeffrey C. **KING**	Aus.401823	RAAF	**A58-109**	VC/Trop	-

During take off which took place at 16.05 for a test flight, P/O King had engine trouble and on reaching the end of the runway he decided to return to base. In making a half circuit he overshot. He then attempted another circuit but lacking power and being too low he had to make a wheels up landing at Hughes Strip. The aircraft caught fire when the belly tank burst into flames as he failed to drop until the last moment. Pilot escaped with burns on one arm. Australian from Victoria, King served in Europe with No.41 Sqn for a short time (August – December 1942) and was repatriated to be posted to No.452 Sqn in March 1943. In December 1943 he was about to complete his tour. He returned to the squadron in April 1945 for another tour and remained with the unit until September when No.452 Sqn was disbanded. Remained with the RAAF after the war.

Note on the aircraft: TOC (RAF) 15.09.42 as EE609, to RAAF arrived Australia 27.11.42. Issued to No.452 Sqn 06.07.43.

01.01.44	F/Sgt Arthur R. **RICHARDSON**	Aus.411644	RAAF	**A58-20**	VC/Trop	-

Hit in rear by Spitfire flown by P/O Etherington after landing at Strauss, escaping injuries. Australian from New South Wales, he had served in Europe for a short while between September 1942 and February 1943 with No.167 Sqn and was then repatriated. He was posted to the Squadron in November 1943 to complete his tour which he did in February 1944. Didn't fly in operations again before the War ended.

Note on the aircraft: TOC (RAF) 11.08.42 as BS295, to RAAF arrived Melbourne, Australia 10.11.42. Issued to No.452 Sqn 24.09.43. Former Clive Caldwell's machine coded 'CRC'.

	P/O Evelyn G.I. **ETHERINGTON**	Aus.403804	RAAF	**A58-111**	VC/Trop	-

Collided with A58-20 flown by F/Sgt Richardson, escaping injuries. Evelyn Etherington was an English-born Australian who flew in England as a recce pilot with No.1 PRU between July and November 1942, then No.140 Sqn between November 1942 and May 1943. At the end of his tour he was repatriated to Australia and joined the squadron in December 1943. He was later killed with the squadron while flying a Wirraway (see entry accident loss Wirraway 20.11.44).

Note on the aircraft: TOC (RAF) 06.10.42 as EE610, to RAAF arrived Melbourne, Australia 23.01.43. Issued to No.452 Sqn 14.12.43. Previously served with No.54 Sqn, RAF.

09.03.44	Sgt Ronald A. **FIVEASH**	Aus.432145	RAAF	**A58-203**	VC/Trop	-

Early in the morning, the squadron had departed for Derby but faced very bad weather. As the weather conditions did not improve, the flight to Derby had to be abandon and the squadron landed at Wyhdham instead. At 14.20, Sgt Fiveash missed the runway on landing at Wyndhamand landed in the mud alongside. The Spitfire nosed over and became trapped in the mud. Extracted not very badly injured but considerably shocked he was taken to Broome Hospital. Fiveash, native of New South Wales, Australia, had joined the squadron the previous January. After a short recovery he returned to the squadron and completed his tour in November that year. In June 1945 he was posted to No.35 Sqn, RAAF as transport pilot.

Note on the aircraft: TOC (RAF) 19.04.43 as JL360, to RAAF arrived Australia 10.08.42. Issued to No.452 Sqn 09.03.43.Previously served with No.54 Sqn, RAF.

11.03.44	F/O Colin H. **O'LAUGHLIN**	Aus.407449	RAAF	**A58-43**	QY-A	VC/Trop	-

Ran out of fuel during ferry flight and force-landed 11m NW of Gin Gin, QLD. [See entry 12.06.44 Operational losses for further details on the pilot].

Note on the aircraft: TOC (RAF) 26.06.42 as BR537, to RAAF arrived Melbourne, Australia 23.10.42. Issued to No.452 Sqn 20.08.43.Previously served with No.54 Sqn, RAF.

31.03.44   F/O Raymond **JOB**   AUS.409702   RAAF   **A58-152**   VC/Trop   -

On that day, F/O Job was instructed to carry out an affiliation flight with a B-24. However, shortly after take-off the bad weather was detected and instructions were given to land. Soon before touching down, the Spitfire dropped suddenly and the aircraft touched the tail wheel first, bounced and then struck a shallow drain which caused the undercarriage to collapse and the aircraft skidded. The pilot sustained slightly injuries. 'Ray' Job had joined the squadron in September 1943 as his first operational posting, having flown as a flying instructor before that. He left the squadron in August at the end of his tour, which was his sole one.

Note on the aircraft: TOC (RAF) 24.02.43 as EF557, to RAAF arrived Australia 02.08.43. Issued to No.452 Sqn 14.09.43.

04.04.44   S/L Louis T. **SPENCE**   AUS.270839   RAAF   **A58-240**   VC/Trop   -

*S/L Spence took off at 19.30 to practice a scramble to intercept a Beaufort with the instructions to land at Darwin on comple tion of the exercise. While on landing, the aircraft swung to starboard and the pilot tried to correct in using brake and rudder without success. The aircraft struck a mound of soft dirt on the edge of the runway causing the aircraft to overturn. When he joined the squadron in February 1944, Spence, who was native of Queensland, Australia, was a very experienced pilot, who had served with No.3 Sqn, RAAF in Middle East he had joined at the end of 1941. Before he served with No.25 Sqn, RAAF in Australia flying Wirraways between October 1940 and August 1941. In June 1942, he left No.3 Sqn, RAAF, tour expi red with two confirmed victories to his credit and a **DFC**. He also distinguished himself in saving one of his squadron mates, Sgt W.H.A. Mailey who had made a forced landing bringing him back to base in his Kittyhawk. He was then repatriated to Australia and was posted as CO of No.452 Sqn for his second tour of operations which ended in December. Louis Spence remained with the RAAF after the war, and was appointed CO of No.77 Sqn, RAAF in Korea. He met his death there on the 9 September 1950 in his Mustang A68-804. He was later awarded a **BAR** to his DFC.*

Note on the aircraft: TOC (RAF) 05.06.43 as MA394, to RAAF arrived Australia 02.08.43. Issued to No.452 Sqn 24.09.43.

24.04.44   Sgt Colin W. **DUNNING**   AUS.437405   RAAF   **A58-232**   VC/Trop   †

Sgt Dunning took off at 15.15 as Blue 2 of a section of four Spitfires for an altitude test. At 25,000 he called up telling that his engine had stopped then had re-started, and began to descend but a couple of minutes later called up again to say that he was facing a glycol leak; he was flying at 1200 feet. He was last seen with engine smoking near Port Patterson (NT) at 15.50, but searches launched in the following days didn't succeed in locating any wreckage. Colin Dunning, age 19, had just joined the squadron early in the month and was a native of South Australia. He was one of the youngest piolt of the unit.

Note on the aircraft: TOC (RAF) 30.05.43 as MA353, to RAAF arrived Australia 02.08.43. Issued to No.452 Sqn 09.03.44.Previously served with No.54 Sqn, RAF.

23.05.44   F/Sgt Hugh S. **McNEIL**   AUS.432834   RAAF   **A58-171**   VC/Trop   -

F/Sgt MacNeil was detailed to carry out an Air to ground gunnery exercise with two other pilots. In putting the throttle back to prepare his turn on the gunnery range, the airscrew went into coarse pitch. The pilot moved pitch forwards and back-wards, but the engine failed to give the needed revs. The pilot had no option but to make an emergency landing which he did on a beach on Governor Island at app. 08.00, pilot uninjured. MacNeil was an Australian from New South Wales, who had joined the squadron in February 1944. He left in January 1945 at the end of his tour and saw no more action with an opera-tional unit until the end of the war.

Note on the aircraft: TOC (RAF) 15.12.42 as JG728, to RAAF arrived Australia 17.05.43. Issued to No.452 Sqn 09.03.44.Previously served with No.457(RAAF)Sqn.

31.05.44   F/Sgt Arthur R. **HEANEY**   AUS.412960   RAAF   **A58-220**   QY-R   VC/Trop   -

Returning from a night training flight, the aircraft swung on landing at Sattler and ran into a bank, pilot escaped injuries. Native of New South Wales, Australia, Heaney had been a Flying instructor for many months when he joined the squadron in February 1944. He eventually completed his tour in November. In September 1945 he joined No.38 Sqn, RAAF, a transport unit. He remained with the RAAF after the war, and served in Japan, leaving the RAAF upon his return to Australia.

Note on the aircraft: TOC (RAF) 19.04.43 as LZ867, to RAAF arrived Australia 10.08.43. Issued to No.452 Sqn 19.10.43.

05.06.44   F/Sgt Arthur R. **HEANEY**   AUS.412960   RAAF   **A58-207**   VC/Trop   -

Returning from a night training flight, the aircraft swung on landing at Strauss and hit a bank, pilot escaped injuries. It was the second accident for F/Sgt Heaney with the same circumstances and causes.

Note on the aircraft: TOC (RAF) 19.04.43 as JL382, to RAAF arrived Australia 03.07.43. Issued to No.452 Sqn 04.04.44.Previously served with No.54 Sqn, RAF.

18.09.44   F/O Arthur K. **Kelly**   Aus.401968   RAAF   **A58-435**   QY-T   LF.VIIIC   †

During an air exercise with B-24s, Kelly collided with a B-24 at about 10.35, striking its port engine with his port wing in a head-on collision. F/O Kelly appeared to have been rendered unconscious by the collision and he made no attempt to correct the airplanes' spin or bale out and the spiralling aircraft crashed into sea 1 m E of Cape Van Diemen, Melville Is (NT). F/O Kelly, native of Victoria, Australia, had joined the squadron four days before and had served with No.277 (ASR) Sqn in England between April 1943 and February 1944.

Note on the aircraft: TOC (RAF) 24.11.43 as JG622, to RAAF arrived Sydney, Australia 18.04.44. Issued to No.452 Sqn 07.07.44.

02.11.44   F/Sgt Barry **O'Connor**   Aus.410134   RAAF   **A58-377**   LF.VIIIC   -

Participating in a dive bombing practice exercise, F/Sgt O'Connor's aircraft suffered an engine failure near Blaze Point and was forced to ditch his aircraft at about 16.20. Escaped with minor injuries and was able to swim to the beach. Australian from Victoria, O'Connor had served previously as flying instructor before joining the squadron in July 1944. He left for No.79 Sqn, RAAF, with which he flew until the end of his tour in June 1945.

Note on the aircraft: TOC (RAF) 09.10.43 as JG267, to RAAF arrived Sydney, Australia 21.01.44. Issued to No.452 Sqn 15.06.44.

01.12.44   F/L Alexander G. **McNaughton**   Aus.416061   RAAF   **A58-401**   LF.VIIIC   -

Took of at 17.00 with three others to ferry Spitfires from Sattler to Gorrie, F/L MacNaughton leading. One hour later the weather deteriorated and the formation was forced to divert to Katherine which was under repair and under water, the ceiling being estimated at 200 feet. While landing, the pilot tried to use the brakes which proved useless due to the water and was unable to stop before reaching an unserviceable patch on the eastern part of the runway. Alexander McNaughton was a former flight instructor. He joined the squadron in August 1944 as supernumerary Flight Lieutenant. Shortly after this accident he was posted to No.457 (RAAF) Sqn for temporary duty until February 1945 and returned to the squadron with which he flew until the end of his tour in June 1945. He was native of South Australia. [see losses by accident 18.12.44 and operational losses 07.03.45].

Note on the aircraft: TOC (RAF) 02.12.43 as MD226, to RAAF arrived Sydney, Australia 29.02.44. Issued to No.452 Sqn 15.07.44.

             F/O Robert L. **Logan**   Aus.412298   RAAF   **A58-450**   LF.VIIIC   -

See above for the circumstances. Was unable to use the brakes and the aircraft skidded along the wet surface with wheels locked and eventually struck a roller. Logan was an Australian from New South Wales who had previously served with No.12 Sqn, RAAF between July 1942 and September 1943. He had joined No.452 Sqn for a second tour in August 1944, he completed in May 1945.

Note on the aircraft: TOC (RAF) 02.12.43 as JG605, to RAAF arrived Sydney, Australia 18.04.44. Issued to No.452 Sqn 16.08.44. Previously served with No.457 (RAAF) Sqn.

17.12.44   F/L Albert L. **Lumley**   Aus.411587   RAAF   **A58-534**   LF.VIIIC   -

On the ferry flight to Morotai, F/L Sturm landed his Spitfire at Merauke and stopped in the middle of the runway at about 10.54. F/O Lumley then landed and tipped the wing of F/L Sturm's Spitfire which was still on the strip at right angles to the runway. F/O Lumley's aircraft had its undercarriage knocked off but was unhurt. It was one of worst accident involving Australian Spitfires. Native of New South Wales, Australia, he completed a first tour with No.131 Sqn in UK between September 1942 and July 1943. He was later repatriated to Australia and joined had joined the squadron a couple days before to finish his second tour he had started with No.457 (RAAF) Sqn in May 1944. He left No.452 Sqn one month later in January 1945.

Note on the aircraft: TOC (RAF) 19.05.44 as MT781, to RAAF arrived Sydney, Australia 27.07.44. Issued to No.452 Sqn 10.12.44.

             P/O William J.H. **Chrystal**   Aus.402729   RAAF   **A58-525**   LF.VIIIC   **Inj.**

As above. P/O Chrystal was the next to land, but had to do it without flaps which had failed. He collided with F/L Sturm's aircraft at relatively high speed unable to avoid it and crashed. He was severely injured. William Chrystal native of New South Wales, Australia, started his operational career in UK flying with No.79 Sqn, RAF in January 1942, then with No.234 Sqn between February 1942 and December 1943, being repatriated the following month. Posted to No.457 (RAAF) Sqn for another tour, then posted to No.452 Sqn in early December 1944. This accident kept him away from any flying duty until the end of war.

Note on the aircraft: TOC (RAF) 27.05.44 as MT550, to RAAF arrived Sydney, Australia 27.07.44. Issued to No.452 Sqn 10.12.44.

             F/L John L. **Sturm**   Aus.407133   RAAF   **A58-478**   LF.VIIIC   †

See above. Killed when P/O Chrystal's aircraft hit his Spitfire while still in the cockpit, the aircraft began to burn after the

collision. 'Johnnie' Sturm, from South Australia, spent two years as flying instructor before joining an operational unit, No.457 (RAAF) Sqn in June 1944. When he was killed he had joined the Squadron early in December with Chrystal and Lumley.
Note on the aircraft: TOC (RAF) 02.03.44 as MT542, to RAAF arrived Melbourne, Australia 13.06.44. Issued to No.452 Sqn 10.12.44. Previously served with No.457(RAAF)Sqn.

18.12.44   F/O Ian A. **Markwell**   Aus.414054   RAAF   **A58-520**   LF.VIIIC   -
That day, F/O Markwell left Merauke for Noemfoor but was forced back due to bad weather. Undercarriage collapsed on landing due to structural failure. Not repaired. Pilot escaped without injuries. [See entry 24.12.44 operational losses for further details on the pilot].
Note on the aircraft: TOC (RAF) 23.04.44 as MT655, to RAAF arrived Melbourne, Australia 15.07.44. Issued to No.452 Sqn 10.12.44.

12.03.45   F/L Alexander G. **McNaughton**   Aus.416061   RAAF   **A58-530**   LF.VIIIC   -
Six aircraft were engaged for a formation practice flight and crashed on landing. At approximately 60-80 mph the pilot felt several severe jars throughout the aircraft as though the undercarriage was collapsing. The pilot then opened the throttle fully in order to clear the runway as two more aircraft were taking off behind him. The increased slipstream lifted the aircraft off the ground for a moment but insufficient flying speed caused it to touch down again quite heavily. (see accident loss entry 01.12.44 for details on the pilot)
Note on the aircraft: TOC (RAF) 27.05.44 as MT703, to RAAF arrived Sydney, Australia 15.07.44. Issued to No.452 Sqn 10.12.44.

22.05.45   F/O Clive R. **Miller**   Aus.420424   RAAF   **A58-533**   LF.VIIIC   †
F/O Miller was BLUE 4 and the seventh member during squadron landing procedure. Approximately at 11.00, undershot during landing and hit a bank of coral and crashed into a mound of earth at the end of the strip, Pitioe, Morotai, and caught fire. Native of New South Wales, Australia, Miller had joined the squadron the previous month. He had flown Wirraways and Boomrangs before flying with No.24 Sqn, RAAF in February 1943, No.83 Sqn, RAAF in April 1943 and eventually with No.85 Sqn, RAAF between May 1943 and February 1945.
Note on the aircraft: TOC (RAF) 22.05.44 as MT778, to RAAF arrived Sydney, Australia 27.07.44. Issued to No.452 Sqn 10.12.44.

14.07.45   F/O John W. **Denhert**   Aus.410149   RAAF   **A58-537**   LF.VIIIC   -
When landing after a test flight, he overshot the runway, crossed a road and turned the aircraft over on its back in a large drain on the opposite side. As his head was submerged in water, he had a fortunate escape when he was able to extricate himself from the cockpit. Denhert was native of Victoria, Australia. He later served the RAAF, post-war.
Note on the aircraft: TOC (RAF) 26.05.44 as MT794, to RAAF arrived Sydney, Australia 27.07.44. Issued to No.452 Sqn 20.10.44.

30.08.45   F/L William M. **Coombes**   Aus.403800   RAAF   **A58-532** QY-W   LF.VIIIC   -
Ditched in sea at about 11.30 during a routine flight after the fuel pressure system failed. [See also operational losses 22.03.43 for details on the pilot]
Note on the aircraft: TOC (RAF) 18.05.44 as MT771, to RAAF arrived Sydney, Australia 27.07.44. Issued to No.452 Sqn 26.12.44.

10.09.45   F/Sgt Daryl **Halliday**   Aus.437786   RAAF   **A58-503** QY-H   LF.VIIIC   -
Crashed on take-off at Tarakan Strip (Croydon strip) when he lost boost. Not repaired. Halliday was native of South Australia and had served with No.85 Sqn, RAAF between June 1944 and May 1945 before joining No.452 Sqn in May. [see also entry 18.10.45, losses by accident]
Note on the aircraft: TOC (RAF) 09.04.44 as MB972, to RAAF arrived Melbourne, Australia 07.07.44. Issued to No.452 Sqn 10.12.44.

18.10.45   W/O Ronald J. **Webb**   Aus.409341   RAAF   **A58-510** QY-U   LF.VIIIC   -
Crashed on landing during a test flight at Croydon strip (Tarakan). Native of New South Wales, Australia, Webb had joined the squadron in May 1945 after a first posting at No.85 Sqn, RAAF between July 1943 and May 1945, flying boomerang, and had served for a short time as flying instructor.
Note on the aircraft: TOC (RAF) 18.03.44 as MT540, to RAAF arrived Sydney, Australia 10.07.44. Issued to No.452 Sqn 10.02.45.

18.10.45   W/O Daryl **HALLIDAY**   Aus.437786   RAAF   **A58-636**   QY-D   HF.VIIIC   -

Crashed on landing during a test flight at Croydon strip (Tarakan). Pilot safe. Aircraft repairable but SOC due to the end of war. [See entry 10.09.45 losses by accident to have more details on the pilot].

Note on the aircraft: TOC (RAF) 24.09.44 as MV170, to RAAF arrived Sydney, Australia 30.11.44. Issued to No.452 Sqn 16.05.45.

RYAN STM

20.10.42   F/L John R. **ROSS**   Aus.400157   RAAF   **A50-21**   -   †
            LAC Walter C. **ELLIOTT**   Aus.14856   RAAF   †

F/L Ross took off at 1545 with LAC Elliott as passenger for an authorised aerobatics flight. Soon after 1600, F/L Ross flew down the runway to examine the surface for the wind had veered since he took off on the longer runway. Near the end of the runway where telephone wires cross the boundary fence the aircraft pulled up fairly steeply. The starboard wing dropped and the pilot tried to regain control. The aircraft seem to begin to spin flatly and to the right while it was at 100 feet and the starboard wing struck the ground. The aircraft nosed over but did not go onto its nose and came to rest 20 yards away in the middle of a shallow pond. Both occupants were rapidly rescued but John Ross died 20 minutes later without regaining conscience while LAC Elliott died the next morning of his wounds. John Ross, from Queensland, Australia was serving the squadron for one year after a brief stay with No.457 Sqn between June and September 41. LAC Elliott, was a native of New South Wales, Australia.

Note on the aircraft: One of 34 Aircraft diverted from an NEI order. TOC 04.08.42. Issued to No.452 Sqn 28.09.42 after having previously served with various training or communication units.

WIRRAWAY

20.11.44   F/O Evelyn G.I. **ETHERINGTON**   Aus.403804   RAAF   **A20-633**   III   †
            F/O Thomas C. **SMITH**   Aus.409008   RAAF   †

F/O 'Buster' Etherintgton was flying with F/O Tom Smith in a Wirraway in a search of a missing mechanic LAC Wise when it crashed in the scrub while circling the land party at their rendezvous near a sawmill. F/O Smith was killed in the crash and 'Buster' Etherington died on the way to the hospital. LAC Wise was found the following day. Smith, native of Victoria, Australia, had joined the squadron in September 1944 for another tour, having completed his first in Europe with No.611 Sqn between December 1942 and February 1944. [As for details for Etherington, see losses by accident 01.01.44].

Note on the aircraft: CA-16.TOC 05.03.44 No.1 AD. Issued to No.452 Sqn 25.05.44.

22.03.45   F/Sgt Colin S. **TAPP**   Aus.420298   RAAF   **A20-235**   II   -
            LAC Raymond M. **REID**   Aus.59306   RAAF   -

While flying at 800 feet, the engine cut without warning. Forced to ditch the aircraft 12 m NE of Pitoe strip. Rescued by natives they returned to the squadron a bit later. Colin Tapp, from New South Wales Australia, completed a full tour with No.452 Sqn, except for three months between December 1944 and February 1945 when he flew with No.457 (RAAF) Sqn for temporary duty. He left the squadron in June 1945. He continued to serve the RAAF after the war. LAC Reid, was a mechanic from Victoria, Australia.

Note on the aircraft: CA-8.TOC 31.03.41 No.1 AD. Issued to No.452 Sqn 20.02.45. Served at various training units between 1941 and 1945.

Total: 51
including 48 combat aircraft

APPENDIX VII
Aircraft serial numbers matching with individual letters

UD-A*/QY-A
BM514*, AR523/A58-2, BS226/A58-90, A58-43 (*Spitfire V*)

UD-B*/QY-B
AR510/A58-1, BS163/A58-62, BS225/A58-89 (*Spitfire V*)

UD-C*/QY-C
P7786* (*Spitfire II*)
BR497/A58-32, EE607/A58-107 (*Spitfire V*)

UD-D*/QY-D
W3821*, BR574/A58-59, BS231/A58-92, A58-227 (*Spitfire V*)
A58-500, A58-636, A58-714 (*Spitfire VIII*)

UD-E*/QY-E
AD242*, BL906*, BS293/A58-101 (*Spitfire V*)
A58-504, A58-516 (*Spitfire VIII*)

UD-F*/QY-F
P8148* (*Spitfire II*)
MA387/A58-238, A58-254 (*Spitfire V*)

UD-G*/QY-G
A58-619 (*Spitfire VIII*)

UD-H*/QY-H
BL351* (*Spitfire V*)
A58-503 (*Spitfire VIII*)

UD-I*/QY-I
A58-540 (*Spitfire VIII*)

UD-J*/QY-J
BR526/A58-34 (*Spitfire V*)
A58-420 (*Spitfire VIII*)

UD-K*/QY-K
BR386/A58-22, BR549/A58-55 (*Spitfire V*)
A58-465, A58-503 (*Spitfire VIII*)

UD-L*/QY-L
W3646*, BS186/A58-74 (*Spitfire V*)
A58-484 (*Spitfire VIII*)

UD-M*/QY-M
AB792* (*Spitfire V*)
A58-496 (*Spitfire VIII*)

UD-N*/QY-N
P9562* (*Spitfire I*)
W3605*, A58-222 (*Spitfire V*)

UD-O*/QY-O
A58-518, A58-720 (*Spitfire VIII*)

UD-P*/QY-P
A58-411 (*Spitfire VIII*)

UD-Q*/QY-Q
A58-719 (*Spitfire VIII*)

UD-R*/QY-R
AB198*, AD517*, AD463*, AD537*, AD563*, A58-220 (*Spitfire V*)

A58-564 (*Spitfire VIII*)

UD-S*/QY-S
BR546/A58-52 (*Spitfire V*)

UD-T*/QY-T
BR241/A58-19 (*Spitfire V*)
A58-435, A58-516, A58-532, A58-652 (*Spitfire VIII*)

UD-U*/QY-U
A58-510 (*Spitfire VIII*)

UD-V*/QY-V
AA935*, A58-43, EE608/A58-108, A58-254 (*Spitfire V*)
A58-430, A58-510 (*Spitfire VIII*)

UD-W*/QY-W
AB140*, AB852*, BS174/A58-68 (*Spitfire V*)
A58-532 (*Spitfire VIII*)

UD-X*/QY-X
A58-427 (*Spitfire VIII*)

UD-Y*/QY-Y
P7853* (*Spitfire II*)
BR240/A58-18 (*Spitfire V*)
A58-646 (*Spitfire VIII*)

UD-Z*/QY-Z
A58-653 (*Spitfire VIII*)

APPENDIX VIII
LIST OF KNOWN PILOTS POSTED OR ATTACHED TO THE SQUADRON

RAAF

J.P. **ADAM**, Aus.404491
R.E. **ANDERSON**, Aus.402337
R. **ARMSTRONG**, Aus.403463
J.C.L. **ARMSTRONG**, Aus.419714
A.L. **BAKER**, Aus.403159
K.M. **BARCLAY**, Aus.403471
J. **BARTON**, Aus.409494
K.D. **BASSETT**, Aus.404558
B. **BAWDEN**, Aus.403306
C.J. **BAXTER**, Aus.400771
R.V. **BAXTER**, Aus.403491
M.J. **BEATON**, Aus.417787
D.R. **BEATIE**, Aus.260639
C. **BEECH**, Aus.426450
P.L. **BEESTON**, Aus.403795
J.T. **BELL**, Aus.403307
G.N. **BELL**, Aus.403711
G.S. **BENSON**, Aus.405818, *NEW ZEALAND*

R.H. **BEVAN**, Aus.402218
A.H. **BIRCH**, Aus.402719
J.H.E. **BISLEY**, Aus.402720
A.M. **BLACKBURN**, Aus.401362
A.G.B. **BLUMER**, Aus.411733
V.P. **BRENNAN**, Aus.404692
R.K. **BRIDLE**, Aus.404675
P.W. **BULLOCK**, Aus.434617
W.M.B. **BURVILL**, Aus.404320
J.R. **BYRNE**, Aus.412386
W.O. **CABLE**, Aus.404495
R.N. **CARMICHAEL**, Aus.409025
C.G.B. **CHAPMAN**, Aus.404198
K.B. **CHISHOLM**, Aus.402150
W.J.H. **CHRYSTAL**, Aus.402729
G.E.S. **CLABBURN**, Aus.205245
M. **CLIFFORD**, Aus.403320
F.A. **COCKER**, Aus.40226
K.L. **COLYER**, Aus.403858, *NEW ZEALAND*
M.F. **COMMONS**, Aus.409468

L.S. **COMPTON**, Aus.408970
W.M. **COOMBES**, Aus.403800
D.J. **CORMACK**, Aus.407412
A.G. **COSTELLO**, Aus.404086
G.S. **COTTEW**, Aus.442522
K.D. **COTTON**, Aus.411484
R.J. **COWAN**, Aus.404087
G.J. **COWELL**, Aus.400967
K.K. **COX**, Aus.400141
C.F. **CRAMPTON**, Aus.404138
K.S. **CROSS**, Aus.403130
N.J. **CULLEN**, Aus.406070
W.R. **CUNDY**, Aus.402732
R.J. **DARCEY**, Aus.408172
S.G. **DAVIDSON**, Aus.432676
G.A. **DEAN**, Aus.409821
J.W. **DENHERT**, Aus.410149
W.J.R. **DENNY**, Aus.417056
J. **DONALD**, Aus.402231
D.F.K. **DOWNES**, Aus.402647

C.R. **Duncan**, Aus.401778
C.W. **Dunning**, Aus.437405
W.D. **Eccleton**, Aus.402232, *NEW ZEALAND*
J.R.H. **Elphick**, Aus.402157
J.M. **Emery**, Aus.407116
E.G.I. **Etherington**, Aus.403803
D.F. **Evans**, Aus.404724
M.J. **Fakhry**, Aus.409137
R.I. **Ferguson**, Aus.402496
R.A. **Fiveash**, Aus.432145
W.H. **Ford**, Aus.401429
K.J. **Fox**, Aus.402330
H.V. **Freckleton**, Aus.402793
W. **Friend**, Aus.403328
K.M. **Gamble**, Aus.403049
L.H. **Gardner**, Aus.421265
R.G. **Gazzard**, Aus.402115
B.M. **Geissmann**, Aus.404334
G.W. **Godwin**, Aus.432550
A.P. **Goldsmith**, Aus.402500
R.A. **Goodhew**, Aus.403332
J.G. **Gould**, Aus.404613
J.F. **Greenfield**, Aus.411898
R.H.W. **Gregory**, Aus.401944
T.L.J. **Gullifer**, Aus.408650
B.F. **Gurney**, Aus.439285
E.S. **Hall**, Aus.403013
D. **Halliday**, Aus.437786
M.W. **Hamilton**, Aus.404726
J.N. **Hanigan**, Aus.402120
W.S. **Hardwick**, Aus.407791
D.R. **Hare**, Aus.423202
F.G. **Harper**, Aus.404664
G.B. **Haydon**, Aus.404100
A.R. **Heaney**, Aus.412960
J.C.L. **Henning**, Aus.411494
D.E. **Hoile**, Aus.437270
R.T. **Holt**, Aus.404103
E.E. **Hutchinson**, Aus.403602
F.J. **Inger**, Aus.8583*
E.P. **Jackson**, Aus.400227
J.R. **Jenkins**, Aus.405210
R. **Job**, Aus.409702
F.R. **Johnson**, Aus.402518
A.S. **Jones**, Aus.407003**
A.K. **Kelly**, Aus.401968
J.C. **King**, Aus.401823
W.J. **Lamerton**, Aus.407900
E.H. **Lee**, Aus.419722
L.A. **Leeming**, Aus.400992
D.E. **Lewis**, Aus.400148
C.P. **Lloyd**, Aus.404690
R.B. **Lloyd**, Aus.431780
R.L. **Logan**, Aus.412298
A.L. **Lumley**, Aus.411587
R.S. **MacDonald**, Aus.270812
E.L. **Mahar**, Aus.33231
C.F.R. **Manning**, Aus.400230
I.A. **Markwell**, Aus.414054
E.V. **Matthews**, Aus.401989

G.A. **Mawer**, Aus.403112
K.B. **May**, Aus.4049318
F.R. **McCann**, Aus.402129
R.G.F. **McClelland**, Aus.404986
V.J. **McFarlane**, Aus.403360
R.J. **McKimm**, Aus.429262
A.C. **McNab**, Aus.405420
A.G. **McNaughton**, Aus.416061
H.S. **McNeil**, Aus.432834
C.E. **Miller**, Aus.420424
I.A.L. **Milne**, Aus.407078
K.L. **Milne**, Aus.407547
E.M. **Moore**, Aus.403357
J.McA. **Morrison**, Aus.402522
I.S. **Morse**, Aus.403358
D.J. **Murray**, Aus.424203
W.E. **Nichterlein**, Aus.416104
I.G. **Nicol**, Aus.431786
J.H. **O'Byrne**, Aus.408022
B.O. **O'Connor**, Aus.410134
C.H. **O'Laughlin**, Aus.407449
P.A. **Padula**, Aus.411813
J.B. **Pauley**, Aus.406261
A.F. **Peacock**, Aus.403371
I.G. **Peacock**, Aus.408240
A.G. **Pilkington**, Aus.406042
K.J. **Preswell**, Aus.419393
J.A. **Pretty**, Aus.409220
A.J. **Proctor**, Aus.418174
P.McA. **Racklyeft**, Aus.412691
L.S. **Reid**, Aus.400735
A.R. **Richardson**, Aus.411644
A.C. **Roberts**, Aus.402007
K.V. **Robertson**, Aus.752
J.R. **Ross**, Aus.400157
A.T. **Ruskin-Rowe**, Aus.411389
J.G. **Sanderson**, Aus.407835
R.F. **Schaaf**, Aus.403208
R.W.G. **Schoon**, Aus.410734
E.H. **Schrader**, Aus.400135
T.W. **Scott**, Aus.402041
H.V. **Shearn**, Aus.406092
M.E. **Sheldon**, Aus.402256
F.P. **Shelley**, Aus.402408
J.W. **Shoesmith**, Aus.421404
R.H.C. **Sly**, Aus.402250
E.L.L. **Sly**, Aus.402810*
T.C. **Smith**, Aus.409008
D.H. **Smith**, Aus.407256
L.T. **Spence**, Aus.270839
R.L. **Sprake**, Aus.408786
R.S. **Stagg**, Aus.407915
E. McL. **Stevenson**, Aus.432589
H.J. **Stevenson**, Aus.438527
M.J. **Stevenson**, Aus.416159
H.W. **Stockley**, Aus.407881
A.R. **Stuart**, Aus.402141
J.R. **Sturm**, Aus.407133
T.A. **Swift**, Aus.408606
C.L. **Swift**, Aus.430415

J.D. **Tamlyn**, Aus.409613
C.S. **Tapp**, Aus.429298
J. **Tapp**, Aus.432907
J.J. **Tevlin**, Aus.401159
R.E. **Thorold-Smith**, Aus.402144
C.A. **Tiller**, Aus.431798
N.M. **Tolhurst**, Aus.430478
K.W. **Truscott**, Aus.400213
A.K. **Try**, Aus.402264
P.D. **Tully**, Aus.404998
F.W. **Turnbull**, Aus.403611
L.H. **Upward**, Aus.402896
L.H. **Utber**, Aus.401552
T.A. **Vance**, Aus.409349
E.V. **Walliker**, Aus.400033
R.E. **Waters**, Aus.408165
A.E. **Watkin**, Aus.405265
R.W. **Watson**, Aus.404714*
C.N. **Wawn**, Aus.400163
R.J. **Webb**, Aus.409341
J.A. **Weger**, Aus.7141
R.H. **Whillans**, Aus.404693
W.J. **Wilkinson**, Aus.404272
R.R. **Williams**, Aus.402675
K.V. **Williams**, Aus.402264
W.D. **Willis**, Aus.400166
F.J. **Young**, Aus.403777

RAF

R.G.V. **Barraclough**, RAF No.66487
R.W. **Bungey**, RAF No.40042, *AUSTRALIA*
B.P. **Dunstan**, RAF No.1256932, *AUSTRALIA*
A.G. **Douglas**, RAF No.70188
R.G. **Dutton**, RAF No.39072
B.E.F **Finucane**, RAF No.41276, *IRELAND*
A.H. **Humphreys**, RAF No.33543
A.F.P. **James**, RAF No.977446, *AUSTRALIA*
P.StJ. **Makin**, RAF No.116507, *AUSTRALIA*
J.M. **Smith**, RAF No.?

*English-born
**Canadian-born

APPENDIX IX
ROLL OF HONOUR
✝

AIRCREW

Name	Service No	Rank	Age	Origin	Date	Serial
ADAM, John Philip	AUS.404491	P/O	30	RAAF	26.09.43	A58-121
BAKER, Allenby Leslie	AUS.403159	P/O	23	RAAF	04.01.42	AB195
CLIFFORD, Michael	AUS.403320	Sgt	25	RAAF	09.10.42	BR471
COSTELLO, Andrew Robert	AUS.404086	Sgt	23	RAAF	05.07.41	P8085
CULLEN, Norman James	AUS.406070	F/L	28	RAAF	10.07.45	A58-518
DUNNING, Colin William	AUS.437405	Sgt	19	RAAF	24.04.44	A58-232
ECCLETON, William Davis	AUS.402232	Sgt	25	(NZ)/RAAF	19.08.41	P8717
EMERY, John Marsh	AUS.407116	Sgt	27	RAAF	08.12.41	AB966
ETHERINGTON, Evelyn Greame Ivor*	AUS.403804	F/O	26	RAAF	20.11.44	A20-633
FORD, William Hendrie	AUS.401429	F/O	24	RAAF	27.02.43	BS175
GAZZARD, Richard George	AUS.402115	Sgt	21	RAAF	19.08.41	AB785
GEISSMANN, Bernard Malcolm	AUS.404334	Sgt	19	RAAF	19.08.41	AD430
GOODHEW, Reginald Alan	AUS.403332	Sgt	23	RAAF	08.05.42	BL351
HAMILTON, Malcolm Wallace	AUS.404726	Sgt	24	RAAF	09.03.42	AA849
HANNIGAN, John Neate	AUS.402120	Sgt	23	RAAF	07.09.41	AB874
HARPER, Francis Gilbert	AUS.404664	Sgt	28	RAAF	15.02.42	P8711
HAYDON, Gerald Barrington	AUS.404100	Sgt	19	RAAF	09.08.41	P8361
HUTCHINSON, Eric Ebworth	AUS.403602	Sgt	26	RAAF	27.01.43	BS184
JACKSON, Edgar Purton	AUS.400227	Sgt	21	RAAF	13.10.41	AB852
KELLY, Arthur Keith	AUS.401968	F/O	22	RAAF	18.09.44	A58-435
LAMERTON, William John	AUS.407900	F/O	23	RAAF	30.06.43	BR241
LEE, Edmund Henry**	AUS.419722	F/O	21	RAAF	15.08.45	A58-650
LEEMING, Leslie Allen	AUS.407992	F/L	30	RAAF	30.06.43	A58-524
LEWIS, Donald Edwin	AUS.400148	P/O	21	RAAF	22.01.42	AB992
MANNING, Charles Frederick Richard	AUS.400230	Sgt	20	RAAF	18.09.41	W3600
MARKWELL, Ian Allison	AUS.414054	F/O	24	RAAF	24.12.44	A58-519
MAWER, Granville Allen	AUS.403112	F/O	23	RAAF	26.09.43	A58-201
MILLER, Clive Everard	AUS.420424	F/O	23	RAAF	22.05.45	A58-533
MOORE, Erci Mervyn	AUS.403357	Sgt	22	RAAF	06.03.43	BS237
McNAB, Alexander Charles	AUS.405420	F/O	24	RAAF	02.05.43	BS225
NICHTERLEIN, Willie Everard	AUS.416104	P/O	23	RAAF	20.06.43	EE607
PROCTOR, Alan James	AUS.418174	F/L	23	RAAF	02.07.45	A58-465
ROSS, John Roberston	AUS.400157	F/L	26	RAAF	20.10.42	A50-21
RUSTIN-ROWE, Anthony Thomas	AUS.411389	F/Sgt	24	RAAF	20.06.43	BS174
SCHRADER, Eric Henry	AUS.400135	Sgt	21	RAAF	06.11.41	AD242
SMITH, Thomas Claude	AUS.409008	F/O	25	RAAF	20.11.44	A20-633
STEVENSON, Edmond McLeod***	AUS.411389	F/Sgt	20	RAAF	14.04.45	A58-419
STURM, John Ridgeway	AUS.407133	F/L	26	RAAF	17.12.44	A58-478
THOROLD-SMITH, Raymond Edward	AUS.402144	S/L	24	RAAF	15.03.43	BS231
WATERS, Raplh Ernest	AUS.408165	Sgt	25	RAAF	10.04.42	BL384
WILLIAMS, Kenneth Victor	AUS.400264	Sgt	25	RAAF	07.09.41	P8716
WILLIS, William Douglas	AUS.400166	P/O	24	RAAF	18.09.41	W3512

*English-born, **Died of wounds sustained on 04.08.45, ***As a PoW

Total: 42
Australia: 41, New Zealand: 1

GROUNDCREW

ELLIOTT, Walter Clarence	AUS.14856	LAC	29	RAAF	21.10.42	A50-21
GORDON, Kenneth William	AUS.140854	LAC	21	RAAF	17.07.45	-
ORPEN, Ronald Charles	AUS.128879	LAC	22	RAAF	15.01.45	-

Total: 3

Australia: 3

Above: Like many Spitfire fighter squadrons formed in 1941, they started working up on Spitfires Mk.Is before becoming operational with Spitfire Mk.IIs. However Spitfire Mk.Vs soon replaced the older models, allowing the squadron to achieve significant results at the end of Summer and Autumn 1941. The Spitfire Mk.II on landing is P7786/UD-C, and was an aircraft regularly flown by Sgt Keith Chisholm, a pilot who became an ace whilst flying with No.452 Sqn. He claimed his first two kills in this aircraft on 09.08.41.

Left, two late arrival at the squadron, AD563 being issued to No.452 Sqn in December 1941 and coded UD-R, replaced at the end of March 1942 by AD537 which was lost on 03.05.42, P/O Lamerton escaping injuries (see entry - operational losses). This Spitfire became the last loss of the squadron in the UK. It seems that most pilots didn't have their own personal mount while in UK. (*Andrew Thomas & Steve Mackenzie*)

Above:
An interesting but unidentified Spitfire Mk.V. This aircraft was damaged in a landing accident on 29.09.41, Sgt Edgar Jackson believed to be the pilot. The starboard leg collapsed and the aircraft was sent for repairs and we can see that the mechanics have begun to remove the 20mm cannons. The lack of serials let think that it could be one of the first Spitfire Mk.V taken on charge by the RAF before the introduction of the new camouflage during Summer 1941, and it is believed that we are talking about W3646, which was victim of a such an accident on that date. (*AWM*)

Left :
When No.452 Squadron was sent to Andras, it inherited all the flying material of No.457 Sqn, including this Spitfire Mk.V which was lost on 08.05.42 in a mid-air collision, fortunately without major consequences for both pilot (see accidental losses). Note that a previous personal nose art has been deleted. Indeed, this aircraft was the mount of the New Zealander ace John A.A. Gibson, and was coded BP-H, even if at first the insignia and kill markings were retained. (*Steve Mackenzie*).

Above: While aircraft of the squadron are taking off, personnel of the base are watching them. In front, Spitfire V W3821/UD-D usually flown by Raymond 'Throttle' Thorold-Smith. (*Steve Mackenzie*)
Below: Spitfire BM514 served a very short time with No.452 Sqn, being issued to the squadron on 12 May a couple of days before the squadron moved on to Australia to defend the country. (*Bill Maudlin via Drew Harrison*).

Above: The first Spitfires taken on charge No.452 Squadron seen at dispersal at the end of 1942, probably at Mascot, NSW. The arrival of these aircraft is very recent as no individual letter have been painted yet. The only Spitfire which can be identified is BS191 issued to No.452 Sqn on 09.11.42. It became 'X' and had a long career with the squadron. During the first weeks of 1943 its regular pilot was F/O William Lamerton, but it was F/L Makin who was in command when it made a forced landing on 02.05.43 after having intercepted Raid 54 over Darwin. The aircraft was repaired and returned to the squadron in October 1943 as A58-78 this time. The aircraft survived the war. (*Bill Maudlin via Drew Harrison*).
Below: Another view of the squadron around end 1942, beginning 1943, before things became serious. Spitfires 'B' and 'M' can be clearly seen in the middle of other Spitfires, Spitfire 'B' was BS163, wrecked in an accident on 22.03.43, while 'M' is not identified as such. (*Bill Maudlin via Drew Harrison*).

Above: Spitfire 'D' seen at Strauss in February or March 1943. The serial is not visible, probably overpainted, so this aircraft is either BS231 in which S/L 'Throttle' Thorold-Smith was killed on 15.03.43 or BR574 which replaced BS231 in the squadron as being aircraft 'D'. (*Bill Maudlin via Drew Harrison*).
Below: A58-254 (MH591) had its undercarriage which collapsed while taxiing at Strauss. It was repaired and coded QY-V this time before being passed on to No.457 in July 1944. It had been allocated to the squadron the previous month at a time when the squadron didn't have much activity. (*Steve Mackenzie*).

Left :
Two RAAF groundcrew are posing in front of aircraft 'K' which was normally BR386 in the beginning of 1943. The letters 'BR' can be seen after the individual letter,. The squadron code letters 'QY' are not painted yet and they will appear around mid-1943. (*Bill Maudlin via Drew Harrison*)

Below left:
Spitfire Mk.Vs in formation somewhere in mid-1943. The squadron code letters 'QY' have been now introduced, but BS233 does not have its individual letter painted on yet while the aircraft behind is AR533/QY-F. Even if each Spitfire taken on RAAF charge had its RAAF serial allocated, the RAF serials were used until about end of summer 1943. (*Spitfire Association*)

Below, an unidentified Spitfire Mk.V/Trop probably in 1944. The serial is not visible but it seems that the RAAF serial is painted on. This aircraft received the question mark instead of an individual letter. (*Spitfire Association*)

Below :
P/O Malcolm 'Junior' Beaton posing in front of his Spitfire Mk.V A58-236 QY-G in Spring 1944. Note the individual letter painted in a black square under the nose. This practice is rather unusual as it is known that the individual letter the was normally painted under the nose in white with no black square like this. (*Steve Mackenzie*).

Above and right:
As being the CO of the squadron, Lou Spence, for most of 1944, he was able to fly on both Spitfire Mk.V and Mk.VIII. He choose the individual letter 'V', first on A58-254, he named 'Rima II'. As mentioned above, this aircraft had been allocated to the squadron as QY-F before being damaged in an accident. Repaired it returned to the squadron and became Spence's personal mount in March 1944. Note that the serial was repainted in black. When the squadron converted definitively into Spitfire Mk.VIII, Lou Spence choose another aircraft namely 'Rima III', A58-430 (right).
(*Steve Mackenzie and Courtesy Aviation Heritage Museum of WA*)

Below right :
No.452 Sqn transitioned to Spitfire Mk.VIII from January 1944, but the conversion took time, the squadron keeping its Spitfire Mk.Vs for operational duties until June 1944. A58-301 was one of the first Spitfire Mk.VIII to have been allocated to the squadron but a for a short time only being on squadron charge for only two weeks from 21.03.44 to 06.04.44 when it was sent to No.54 Sqn. However, it is not known who flew this aircraft which was christened 'Nancy', nor if an individual letter was assigned to it as it may have flown like this; as the first Spitfire VIII were only used for training. Indeed, those early issue Mk.VIIIs were withdrawn after a few weeks as they had major problems (corrosion issues and improperly sealed fuel tanks that were stopping them from giving full performance). They preferred to stick with the Mk.Vs until the problems were fixed.
(*Bill Maudlin via Drew Harrison*).

Above: Spitfire LF.VIII A58-43/QY-T was flown by William 'Ron' Cundy in 1944. When he joined the squadron, he was a very experienced pilot who had flown Kittyhawks with No.260 Sqn in the Middle East with which he claimed seven confirmed victories, two being shared, and had been awarded a DFM and a DFC. Unfortunately he didn't have the opportunity to make more kills while flying in the Pacific and ended the war with an unchanged tally. Note the Pegsaus painted ahead of the cockpit, a symbol regularly used with variants on Spitfires of No.80 Fighter Wing, as many variants of this Pegasus have been noted. (*Steve Mackenzie*)
Below: Squadron's Spitfire Mk.VIIIs flying on formation at the end of 1944. The Spitfire Mk.VIII is often seen as being the best Spitfire variant but this mark didn't have the opportunity to prove this in the SWPA. When it was introduced in Australia in 1944, the Japanese aircraft were no more a threat for Australia, and the American gave just enough space to the other Allied air forces and the RAAF in particular to be symbolically there, but enough not to be very essential.
(*Courtesy of Aviation Heritage Museum of WA*).

Above, two Spitfires LF.VIIIC under maintenance at Morotai in July 1945, A58-504 coded 'R' and A58-540 coded 'I', a letter rarely used. Note that each one wears a personal insignia ahead of the cockpit, a regular practice as far as it is known especially for the Spitfire VIIIs. On the left, A58-504, a Spitfire regularly flown by 'Rex' Watson. He chose the Disney character 'Jiminy Cricket' which appears in all his known Spitfires even if the drawing may be different. Note also the three Japanese Navy flags painted ahead of the cockpit for the three victories he claimed against the Japanese.

Below, another side view of Watson's A58-504 with its 'Jiminy Cricket' Disney character painted ahead of the cockpit, with the fin flash and with a different style of letter codes. It seems that this photo was taken before the one above. (*Courtesy Aviation Heritage Museum of WA*)

Some views of Spitfires at Morotai during Summer 1945. A58-532/QY-W, a Spitfire LF.VIIIC which was issued to No.452 Sqn on 26.12.44 and was lost in a flying accident on 30.08.45 (see accidental losses). QY-D was another Spitfire Spitfire LF.VIIIC, A58-500, which was previously used by No.54 Sqn, RAF before being allocated to the squadron on 10.12.44. The spinner is normally red, with the 'Ace of Spades' insignia on rudder.
(*Steve Mackenzie*)

Below, for sure a nice place for a tourist, but in July 1945 Balikpapan was a war zone, but this photograph gives a good idea of the environment the personnel had to live with. The Spitfire are seen here at dispersal, the only aircraft which can be identified is QY-G/A58-619, a Spitfire HF.VIIIC which arrived at the squadron in May 1945. This aircraft was not sent back to Australia, probably because it was grounded when the squadron was repatriated and its remnants were left behind after the war's end. There are many interesting things to notice, the spinners are now white, even if on the left side one Spitfire has still its spinner painted in red. Behind, another Spitfire is covered with a canvas sheet, and still has its RAF fin flash while it has received the 'Ace of Spades' on the rudder and all RAAF roundels!

Like many Article XV squadrons, the command of the squadron and the flights were given to RAF officers during the first months after their formation. As far as possible they were native from the Dominion the squadron was raised from with the aim to facilitate relationship between the pilots and the leaders of the squadron.

No.452 Sqn was first led by Roy Dutton - top left - a Battle of Britain veteran (see biography p15) followed by Bob Bungey - bottom left, an Australian serving in the RAF. He fought as a Fairey Battle pilot with No.226 Sqn in France and volunteered to serve in Fighter Command during the Battle of Britain fighting with No.145 Sqn, with which he claimed two shared confirmed victories, and being shot down once. After he left the squadron with one more confirmed victory to his tally and a DFC, he did not fly in operations again, having various staff postings and eventually transferred to the RAAF in January and repatriated to Australia. He died there on 10.06.43 in non military circumstances. (*Spifire Association*)

Arguably the most charismatic pilot of the early days was 'Paddy' Finucane DFC - right - an Irish pilot who fought during the Battle of Britain. His legend was actually born while serving with the squadron claiming the majority of his 32 confirmed victories (6 being shared), and was awarded the only DSO of the squadron and a Bar to his DFC. He left the 452 to take command of 602 Sqn and later became CO of Hornchurch wing. He died in action on 15.07.42.

A handful of No.452 Sqn pilots posing in September 1941 for the camera, L-R:
Sgt Clive 'Bardie' Wawn, Sgt John R. Ross who has been recently posted in from No.457 (RAAF) Sqn, Sgt J. M. Smith, RAF (sitting), who left the squadron soon after, Sgt Francis Harper, Sgt Malcolm Hamilton, Sgt William Wilkinson and Sgt Raife Cowan, the two latter being just posted from No.457 Sqn. Harper and Hamilton were both killed in UK a few weeks later and when Ross returned to Australia, he became the first pilot to lose his life after the return of the 452 squadron. Wawn survived the war serving with No.76 Sqn, RAAF in returning to Australia. He had served previously with Nos.111 and 92 Sqns in UK.
(*Steve Mackenzie*)

Group portrait of pilots of No.452 Sqn in the beginning of 1942. Left to right: P/O 'Jack' Elphick, P/O Robert Armstrong, both surviving the war, S/L Keith W. Truscott recently appointed CO killed in March 1942, P/O Mark E. Sheldon killed on 11.08.42 with No.76 Sqn RAAF; F/L Raymond H. C. Sly who was killed in Malta the day of his arrival on 09.05.42 and P/O Davidson F. Evans.

Keith 'Bluey' Truscott (left) was probably the most publicised Australian fighter pilot in 1941-1942. Enlisted in the RAAF in July 1940, he was trained in Canada and joined the 452 on formation in May 1941. During Summer and Autumn 1941, he became one the most successful Australian pilot of the squadron and more generally in UK and was naturally chosen to lead a Flight and later the squadron. In need of experienced pilots to defend the Country against the Japanese, the RAAF decided to send him back to Australia in March 1942 where he received a hero's welcome. Because of his great popularity he was allowed to retain his Squadron Leader rank without commanding any squadron, as no vacancies were available at that time, and fought with No.76 Sqn, RAAF as supernumerary Squadron Leader at first, later commanding the squadron after Peter Turnbull's death. Before being killed on 28 March 1943 in a flying accident, he was able to add one confirmed kill to his 14 German kills (one being shared), making a grand total of 15.

(Courtesy Aviation Heritage Museum of WA)

Ray 'Throttle' Thorold-Smith (right) was another great Australian personality of the 452. Enlisted in May 1940 and trained in Canada like Truscott, he joined the squadron one year later in April 1941. Within a year he rose to the rank of Squadron Leader and became the CO after the departure of Truscott in March 1942. He was the one who brought back the 452 to Australia and who led the 452 in the first actions against the Japanese as part of the 'Churchill' Wing. However he was killed during his second sortie against the Japanese, a very sad loss for the 452 and for the wing as well who had lost a very experienced pilot after shooting down 7 enemy aircraft, one being shared. *(Steve Mackenzie)*

Above, some early pilots of the squadron in 1941, L-R: Sgt 'Alex' Roberts, 'Dick' Gazzard, 'Paddy' Finucane, 'Bluey' Truscott, 'Ian' Milne and 'Fred' McCann. All survived the war but Finucane, Truscott and Gazzard, the latter on 19.08.41 while serving the squadron.
Below, return of mission at the end of summer 1941 for F/L Alfred Douglas (with gloves), at that time still B Flight Commander, surrounded by, left to right, Sgt 'Ros' Stagg, 'Ray' Sly, and Mark Sheldon with the Mae West. Sheldon would be killed the following year on 11.08.42 while serving 75 Sqn, RAAF.

Above, some more early pilots of the squadron in 1941, L-R: Bruce Dunstan, who was later posted to No. 41 and killed in action in February 1942, 'Ian' Milne in the door step, Keith Chisholm, 'Jack' Elphick (partially hidden by Chisholm), 'Don' Lewis († 22.01.42), Bluey Trsucott, Clive Wawn and Raife Cowan.
Below, another scene when pilots are 'killing the time'. Those identified are L-R: 'Throttle' Thorold-Smith, 'Ross' Stagg, Sgt St-J Makin (an Australian serving in the RAF), 'Don' Lewis and 'Will' Willis who would be killed on 18.09.41.

Above: Group portrait of No.452 Sqn at Andreas in Spring 1942, shortly before moving to Australia. Left to right: Sgt Ronald H. Bevan, Sgt Kenneth D. Bassett; P/O Davidson F. Evans, Sgt Eric M. Moore, Sgt Henry W. Stockley, Sgt Paul D. Tully, Sgt Ross S. Stagg. At that time, No.452 Sqn had taken over No.457 Sqn's role of advanced OTU, and except for, Bevan, Bassett and Moore, all the others were new comers. Bevan had been trained with No.457 Sqn the previous summer before joining the squadron while Evans ended up serving with No.457 Sqn by the end of the war. All while serving with the squadron survived the war except for Moore.

Below, another group of pilots, at the same place and at the same time. Left to right:
P/O William J. Lamerton, P/O David F.K. Downes, S/L 'Throttle' Thorold-Smith the CO, F/L Paul St. J. Makin and P/O Reginald R. Williams. Lamerton and Thorold-Smith were both later killed while serving the squadron, while the other three survived the war. (*Steve Mackenzie*)

Above, Strauss, NT 25 April 1943, just before the beginning of the fierce weeks of combat in Spring 1943 over Darwin. Left to right:
Back row: F/O John P. Adams, F/O Reginald R. Williams, F/Sgt Frederick 'Darky' McDowell of No.457 Sqn (†06.07.43 with No.457 Sqn); Wing Commander Clive R. 'Killer' Caldwell commanding the 1st Fighter Wing comprising alongside 452 Sqn, No.457 (RAAF) Sqn and No.54 Sqn, RAF, F/O Adrian 'Tim' Goldsmith a former Malta veteran DFC DFM and an ace with over 14 victories to his credit at that time, F/L Edward S. Hall, Sergeant Colin R. Duncan.
Front row: Sgt Frederick C. White, F/O John G. Gould F/Sgt Paul D.Tully.

Below, another photo during the raids over Darwin, shortly after the arrival of the new CO Ronald MacDonald (last at right), also seated are 'Killer' Caldwell. L-R: 'Tim' Goldsmith, Sgt William Coombes who survived the war, retiring as RAAF Wing Commander in 1968 and John Adams. (*Greg Callaghan via M. Laird*)

Photo of members in posting in June 1944, while the 452 was stationed at Sattler, NT.
With Malcolm 'Junior' Beaton seated on the prop, on back row, left to right:
Ross S. Stagg, Alan S. Jones, Peter W. Bullock, David J. Murray, Fred R. Johnson, William 'Ron' Cundy, Louis T. Spence (CO), Keith M. Gamble, Alan J. Proctor, Ronald S. MacDonald, Ray Job, Ken V. Robertson, Jack G. Sanderson.
Front Row: L-R, John H. Greenfield, Rex L. Sprake, Arthur R. Heaney, Harry 'Bill' Stevenson, Col S. Tapp, Francis G.F. Hatten (groundcrew), Tom W. Scott, Noel M. Tolhust, Hugh S. MacNeil, Doug E. Hoile, Colin H. O'Loughli. (*Spitfire Association*)

Below, at Morotai, Halmahera Islands, NEI, four pilots are standing in front a Spitfire VIII in January 1945.
Left to right:
W/O John R. Byrne, F/L Lyndon S. Compton, F/L Thomas A. Swift and F/L Desmond J. Cormack, B Flight leader at that time. All survived the war. Compton had served in Europe flying with No.124 Sqn, and served briefly with 452 Sqn's sister unit, No.457 for a short in 1944. He remained with the RAAF after the war.

Balikpapan, Borneo, in July 1945 some pilots are posing for posterity at Sepinggang airstrip. Left to right:
F/L Jack A. Pretty, 'A' Flight CO, F/L Robert N. Carmichael, F/O Rex W. Watson, W/O Clive L. Swift, F/Sgt Brian F. Gurney and F/O Joseph A. Weger. Gurney, Swift, Watson and Weger had all served with No.457 Sqn before, No.452 Sqn's sister unit. Watson fought with No.457 Sqn during the critical weeks of 1943 over Darwin and claimed two Zekes destroyed, while Weger had also served with No.457 Sqn in the same time but as ground staff, being later accepted for a pilot course. (*Author's collection*). Below right, two pilots who became B Flight commanders, from left to to right John Bisley and William Cundy (*Spitfire Association*).

Two very experienced pilots led No.452 Sqn during the war. Above, Louis T. Spence had served with No.3 Sqn, RAAF in Middle East when he was awarded the DFC. He remained with the RAAF after the war, and was appointed CO of No.77 Sqn, RAAF in Korea and met his final fate in action there on the 9 September 1950 flying his Mustang A68-804. He was later awarded a Bar to his DFC. Right, Below, Kevin Barclay was the only Australian to have served in three Australian squadrons raised under Article XV regulations, No.453 Sqn in Europe, with which he gained a DFC, and Nos.452 & 457 Sqns in SWPA. He flew 150 sorties in Europe with No.453 Sqn but also with Nos.32 & 66 Sqns. He served with RAAF after the war. (*Steve Mackenzie & Author's*).

Squadron Leader Arthur Birch posing in front of a Squadron's Spitfire in Spring 1945. (via Spitfire Association)

Summary of the operational activity
No.452 (R.A.A.F.) Squadron

A/C types	First sortie	Last sortie	Total sorties	Lost Ops	Lost Acc	A/C lost	Claims	Pilot †	PoWs	Eva.
Spitfire I	-	-	-	-	1	1	-	-	-	-
Spitfire II	22.05.41	27.08.41	453	5	1	6	16.0	2	2	1
Spitfire V	10.08.41	12.06.44	[1]1,684	39	31	70	73.0	28	4	-
Spitfire VIII	22.12.44	10.08.45	978	12	15	27	2.0	8	1	-
Others										
Other causes	-	-	-	-	-	-	-	[2]1	-	-
Ryan STM	-	-	-	-	1	1	-	1	-	-
Wirraway	-	-	-	-	2	2	-	2	-	-
Compilation	22.05.41	10.08.45	3,115	56	51	107	91.0	42	7	1

[1] The figures for Europre are 972 sorties, 19 combat losses, 8 accidental losses and 53.0 claims.

[2] Died in a PoW camp.

Main awards

DSO: 1

DFC: 9

Including 1 Bar and 1 Second Bar

DFM: 1

Points of interest :
- First RAAF fighter squadron formed in Fightrer Command.

Unsolved mystery
Service number of Sgt J.M. Smith, RAF, with the squadron in 1941.

Statistics :
- Lost one aircraft every 55 sorties (Spitfire II - 90; Spitfire V - 43 [51 for Europe and 35.6 for Australia/SWPA]; Spitfire VIII - 81.5).
- 46.15 % of the combat aircraft losses occured during non operational flights, a very high rate for a fighter unit.

BADGE

On a circle white label background a roundel gules bordered au and placed within the outer stars of the Crux Australis au arranged on the white label background and bearing centrally a winged Kookaburra volant to the dexter with a sprig of wattle slipped proper (Acacia Australis) above.

The Kookaburra is a kingfisher indigenous to Australia.

MOTTO

MUNDUS PRO NOBIS

- THE WORLD BEFORE US -

Supermarine Spitfire Mk.IIA P7786, Sgt Keith B. Chisholm, Kenley, July 1941.
Taken on charge on 16.12.40, P7786 served with No.303 (Polish) Sqn before being issued to No.452 Sqn on 21.05.41 and became Keith Chisholm's mount from the beginning. He claimed his first two and only kills on Spitfire Mk.II flying P7786 on 09.08.41. Like on many fighters in 1941, the serial number had been partially over-painted when the fuselage band was introduced at the end of 1940. Note the oversized underwing roundel (see p.26).

Supermarine Spitfire Mk.VB W3646, Sgt Edgar P. Jackson, Kenley, 29 September 1941.
Taken on charge on 05.08.41 at No.5 MU, it was painted with a Dark Earth/Dark Green in use until 15.08.41 and was issued to No.452 Sqn on 16.08.41. When the new Fighter Command camouflage with the Ocean Grey was introduced in mid-August, W3646 was then repainted at the squadron and the serial number overpainted. This aircraft which can been seen p27, was damaged in a landing accident at Kenly when its starboard leg collapsed. Its pilot, Sgt Jackson, had joined the squadron a couple of days before and was performing one of his first flights with the squadron and was not operational yet. W3646 was repaired and eventually converted as a Seafire Mk.IB (NX965), its pilot, Sgt Jackson was less fortunate and was killed during his first operational sortie one month later. The artwork could not be identified with certainty, probably a kind of Bigfoot as shown, but it can't be associated to any pilot W3646 having flown 10 operational sorties with the 452 in the hands of at least half a dozen pilots.

AB198

UD·R

- SNIFTER-II -

- SNIFTER-II -

Supermarine Spitfire Mk.VB AB198, Andreas, May 1942.

Taken on charge on 11.12.41 at No.5 MU, it was a presentation aircraft named 'CENTRAL PROVINCES AND BERAR IV'. it served with Nos.134 and 81 Sqns before being officially issued to No.452 Sqn on 05.05.42. The aircraft served a month with the squadron until the latter left for Australia in June and AB198 did not have the opportunity to carry out many operational flights – 2 only! When the aircraft arrived at the squadron, its name was deleted and replaced by another artwork, an Australian popular pre-war 'Snifter' after Hardmuth Lahm's character. This aircraft was the second Spitfire V to have such a dog painted on its fuselage, a previous UD-R being known to have been existed, hence the surname 'Snifter II'.

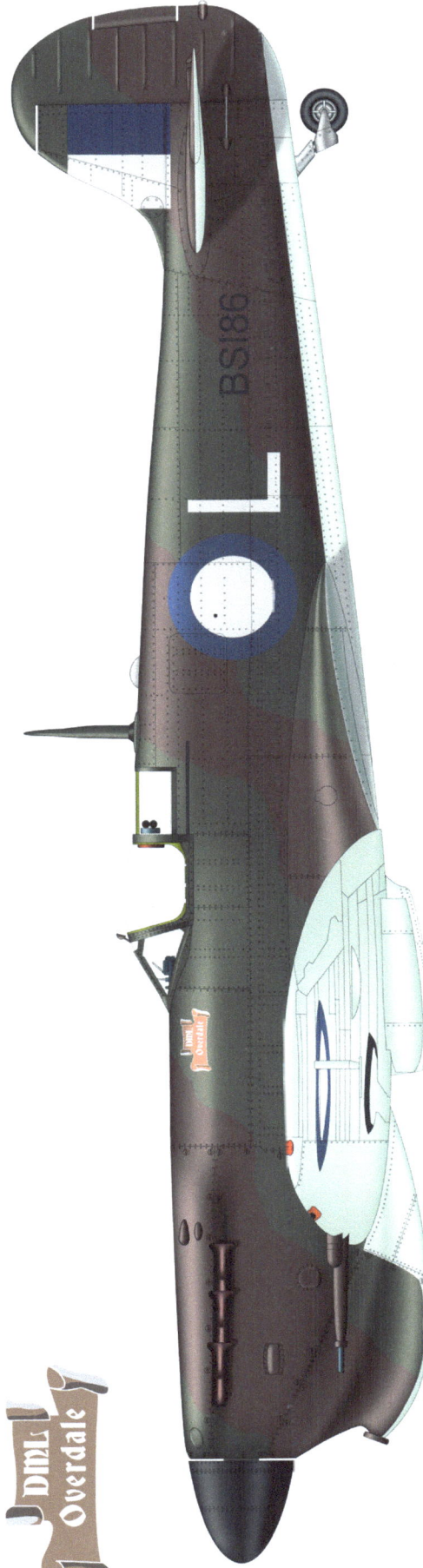

BS186

·L

DML Overdale

Supermarine Spitfire Mk.VC/Trop BS186, F/L Edward 'Sammy' Hall, Strauss (NT), Australia, March 1943.

Taken on RAF charge on 07.07.42 as MA366, this aircraft reached Melbourne, Australia on 23.10.42 and was issued to No.452 Sqn the following month as being one of the first Spitfires to be allocated to the squadron. Coded 'L', it became the mount of A Flight leader, 'Sammy' Hall with which he claimed one confirmed victory on 6th June and named his aircraft 'D.M.L. Overdale'. 'Sammy' Hall had served with No.129 Sqn in Europe before joining the squadron in January 1943. He left in July and never served in operations again being released from the service in November 1944. During the first half of 1943, only the individual letter was worn, the squadron code letters 'QY' appearing in mid-1943, painted in sky blue. Later during the year and by Autumn 1943, the RAAF serial system replaced the RAF one, and BS186 was re-serialled A58-74. BS186 was painted in Temperate scheme.

Supermarine Spitfire Mk.VC/Trop A58-236, P/O Malcolm J. 'Junior' Beaton, Sattler (NT), Australia, April 1944.

Taken on RAF charge on 09.06.43 as MA366, this aircraft reached Australia on 02.08.43 and was re-serialed A58-236. Repaired it was then issued to No.54 Sqn, RAF in November 1943, but was damaged in an accident on 23th December. It was then issued to No.452 Sqn on 06.04.44 and was then regularly flown by 'Junior' Beaton who served with the squadron between September 1943 to August 1944 (see p32). The aircraft is camouflaged with the Standard Temperate scheme. Note that the tropical filter cowling contrary to A58-254 is not painted with the upper surfaces colours but with the Sky colour of the undersurfaces. Note the individual letter 'G' painted in green square. The square was an unusual practice with this squadron as the individual letter was more often painted in sky blue. Like A58-254 when the squadron switched definitively to Spitfire Mk.VIII models, A58-236 was passed on to No.457 Sqn in July 1944 and eventually survived the war.

Supermarine Spitfire Mk.VC/Trop A58-254, S/L Louis T. Spence, Sattler (NT), Australia, March 1944.

Taken on RAF charge on 08.08.43 as MH591, this aircraft was named 'RIMA II'. It reached Australia on 21.10.43 and was re-serialed A58-254. Repaired it returned to the squadron the following month to become the personal mount of the CO, who added the Squadron Leader pennant under the cockpit and choose this nickname (see p32 & 41). The aircraft is camouflaged with the Standard Temperate scheme with Medium Sea Grey undersurfaces. Note that the tropical filter cowling is also painted with the upper surfaces colours and it is believed that the individual letter is also painted on its front. When the squadron switched definitively to Spitfire Mk.VIII models, A58-254 was passed on to No.457 Sqn in July 1944. A58-254 and survived the war.

Supermarine Spitfire LF.VIIIC A58-301, Strauss, NT Australia, April 1944.

Built as JF621 and taken on RAF charge on 14.08.43, A58-301 arrived at Melbourne, Australia on 21.10.43. It was the second RAAF Spitfire Mk.VIII. Photos of the first Spitfire VIIIs issued to SWPA operational squadrons are rare and especially this A58-301 which served with No.452 Sqn for two weeks only between 21.03.44 and 06.04.44 when it was sent to No.54 Sqn (see p32). In April 1944, No.452 Sqn was still flying on Spitfire Mk.Vs and flew all its few operations in Spring 1944 on that type and none of Spitfire VIIIs, so we can imagine that the few Spitfires VIIIs received in early 1944 were used only for training purpose as the early Spitfire VIIIs had some technical trouble. That could explained why no individual letter was allocated, but it was in another hand it was christened 'Nancy'. The camouflage is believed to be Foliage Green/Darl Earth/Azure blue with the white leading edge bands as code letters, the serial painted in Medium Sea Grey. The spinner can't be seen on the photo, but it is thought to be black.

Supermarine Spitfire LF.VIIIC A58-516, F/O Kenneth B. May, Morotai (NEI), December 1944.

Built as JG690 and taken on RAF charge on 06.04.44, this Spitfire arrived at Sydney, Australia on 17.07.44 where it became A58-516 and was issued to No.452 Sqn on 10.12.44. It was probably flown by F/O Ken May the only pilot who had claimed two Japanese aircraft by December 1944, claims he made while serving with No.79 Sqn, RAF in Burma in 1942. The aircraft was later damaged in an accident on 12.04.45 but returned to the squadron in June 1945 as QY-E. This Spitfire is fully painted with RAAF Foliage Green, RAAF Blue for the undersurfaces with the Red spinner which was the quick identification markings for the 452 Sqn, while the leading edges in white the Ace of Spades painted on the rudder identify No.80 Wing. This aircraft was eventually wrecked by F/Sgt Brian Gurney in July.

53

Supermarine Spitfire LF.VIIIC A58-504, F/O Rex W. Watson, Tarakan (NEI), July 1945

Built as MB974 and taken on RAF charge on 09.04.44, this Spitfire arrived at Melbourne, Australia on 07.07.44. Issued to No.452 Sqn on 10.12.44 and was flown by various pilots before becoming the regular mount of Rex Watson when he joined the squadron in April 1945. As on all his aircraft, Rex Watson painted around the cockpit a 'Jiminy Cricket' of Disney fame. As shown on photos p.34, this aircraft seems to have seen its squadron codes letters and individual letter repainted at some stage with a new style, here being the one appearing around July 1945. An oddity, this aircraft is regularly reported as A58-564 on the ORB, a sequence number which was never used in the RAAF inventory. The reason of the lack of the fin flash is not known, neither of the aircraft flew like this. The paints are standard for that period, Foliage green/Sky blue. Note the three Japanese Navy flags painted ahead of the cockpit for the three Watson's confirmed claims he claimed while serving with No.457 (RAAF) Sqn. The spinner is red, a colour widely used on No.452 Sqn aircraft even if by that time, white spinner is often seen. Note the spinner back plate is still painted on RAF Sky as it was received from the RAF.

Supermarine Spitfire HF.VIIIC A58-646, Tarakan (NEI), July 1945

Built as MV474 and taken on RAF charge on 17.09.44, this Spitfire arrived at Sydney, Australia on 30.11.44 where it became A58-646. Issued to No.452 Sqn on 02.07.44 it was flown by various pilots during the last weeks of the war, including F/L 'Blue' Colyer (NZ) and F/Sgt Daryl Halliday, both being the two who flew the most A58-646. This Spitfire had kept the RAF Dark Green/Ocean Grey camouflage as many Australian Spitfires of the last batches, but surprisingly it also kept the RAF fin flash and seems to have flown like this, at least during the first days of July 1945. The spinner is white as the letter codes.

SQUADRONS! No.3

Fighter Leaders
of the RAF, RAAF, RCAF, RNZAF & SAAF in WW2

Volume I
Phil H. Listemann

Volume II
Phil H. Listemann

USN AIRCRAFT 1922-1962
Vol. 2: Designation Letter

RAF, Dominion & Allied Squadrons at War: Study, History and Statistics

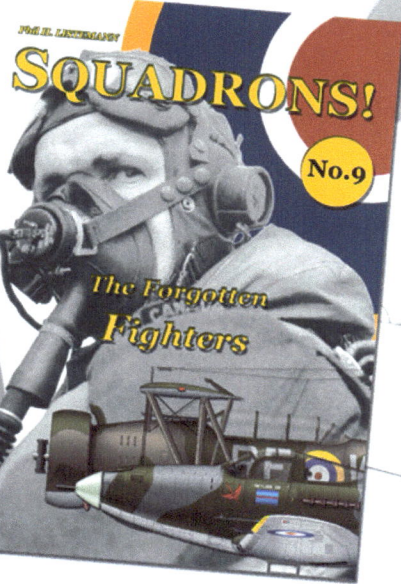

No.137 Squadron 1941 - 1945

SQUADRONS! No.10
The North American Mustang Mk. IV in Western Europe

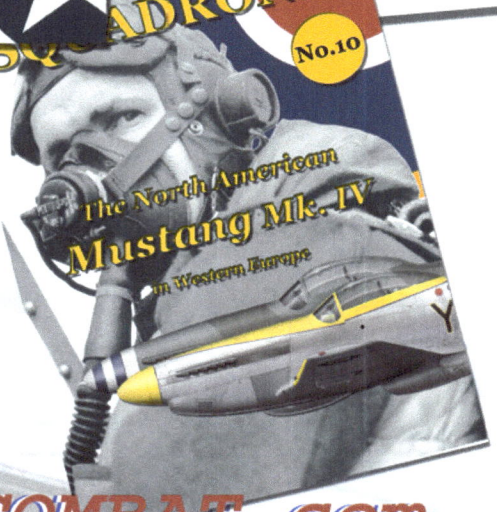

www.RAF-IN-COMBAT.com

- USN Aircraft 1922-1962 -
- Squadrons! -
- RAF, Dominion and Allied squadrons at War -
- Allied Wings -
- Famous squadrons of WW2 -
- Fighter Leaders -

No.453 (R.A.A.F.) Squadron 1941-1945
Buffalo, Spitfire

No.131 (County of Kent) Squadron 1941 - 1945

SQUADRONS! No.9
The Forgotten Fighters

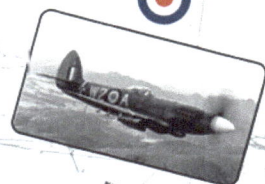

ALLIED WINGS
No.18
The Supermarine SPITFIRE F.24
Phil H. Listemann

www.ingramcontent.com/pod-product-compliance
Lightning Source LLC
Chambersburg PA
CBHW060813090426
42737CB00002B/56